Store Windows That Sell

BOOK 4

Store Windows That Sell

BOOK 4

Edited by Martin M. Pegler, SVM

RETAIL REPORTING CORPORATION • *New York*

Retail Reporting Corporation, 101 Fifth Avenue
New York, NY 10003

Distributors to the trade in the United States and Canada:
Robert Silver Associates
307 East 37th Street
New York, NY 10016

Distributed outside of the United States and Canada:
Hearst Books International
105 Madison Avenue
New York, NY 10016

Library of Congress Cataloging in Publication Data:
Main Entry under the title: Store Windows That Sell, Book 4

Printed in Hong Kong
ISBN 0-934590-27-3

Designed by Bernard Schleifer

Contents

BLOOMINGDALE'S, *Lexington Avenue, New York City*
V.M. Director: **Colin Birch, V.P.**

Introduction

High Tech has created an "art" out of the mundane—the mass produced, often industrial materials that we find around us but rarely "see". It has taken the usual and made it unique; it has found "beauty" in the form that follows function and that also serves purpose.

This book is, in a way, dedicated to High Tech. We have searched out exciting, stimulating and selling displays that also utilize the things we take for granted—and elevates them to distinctive and distinguished props—to visual statements that help make merchandising statements in their in-the-spotlight location. These are not the expensive props that can make a gaping hole in the display budget, but the things that are all around us—possibly in our own stores as stock, or in our stock-rooms as crating materials or disposable "trash"—or even the trash cans that hold the material about to be discarded. These "things" are in the stores and shops that surround us in the mall or strip center—or in the stores down the street that sells the luggage we don't sell—or the office supplies we don't carry—the hardware or garden supplies that are not part of our inventory. However, out of their usual milieu and into the well lit, clean and professionally prepared fashion display space—inside the store or out in the window—those refrigerators, electric fans, vacuum cleaners and up-ended terra-cotta flower pots become the eye-grabbing, attention-getting, message-relating display props that make a display stand out and reach out to the shoppers.

This volume is a paean to the prop—the budget stretching kind—the ones one can find from the rubbish room, pick up and paint up for pennies from a Salvation Army outlet—borrow for a credit card in the window from the appliance store down the road—or salvage from a garage sale or a house razing. Some of our props may be a bit more "costly" but they live on eternally in the effective display department and never get "tired" or "passe". Things like columns, capitols, plaster busts or classic sculptures, and picture frames of every size and degree of ornateness have myriad uses; they adapt to so many classifications of merchandise—can be used in so many ways and never look exactly the same. Many of these, too, can be "borrowed" from art supply stores, antique shops, galleries—or even lumber yards.

We hope you will be stimulated by our Primer of Props—the ABC's of Everyday Decoratives that can add a new dimension—excitement and drawing power to your displays, and you'll try the "Beg—Borrow & Credit Card" approach to Store Windows That Sell.

Martin M. Pegler, SVM

1
Backroom and Out in the Street

This is a book about "Found Art"—about everyday objects that surround us and that we take for granted—that suddenly take on new meaning—provide understanding and make contact with viewers outside. They gain in stature by becoming display props and add their new found status to the merchandise being displayed. This book is a celebration of the ordinary and the mundane used in unique and unusual ways to become special and make special the merchandise they share the scene with.

Not everything is "found"—some we must buy but much can be borrowed or rented. However, before we step out to "shop" the stores that are all around us—where these "props" are commonly found, let us start in our own shop and see what "treasures" we can uncover in our own back room—our receiving and shipping department—the basement or the attic. On the next several pages we have some interesting and intriguing uses of brown wrapping paper—kraft paper—tissue—of cartons, crates and twine—of the materials in which we receive our deliveries and the boxes, bags and garment bags in which we send the merchandise out of the store. The latter group are special salespersons. They carry our names out of the store—into the street—for all to see. Why not use some of your own special, monogrammed materials to dress a window or a mannequin for an "Everything Must Go" sale. Pack your shopping bags—stuff them full with sale merchandise—or let your mannequins carry their own visible coordinates and accessories.

All those wire hangers that you hate to untangle—that manage to enmesh in one another—can become mobiles or stabiles that float overhead—or cascade down to the floor. With good lighting and a back panel behind them they will create fantastic shadow patterns. The wooden or heavy plastic hangers can be artfully arranged into designs or can appear haphazardly tossed about in a window without merchandise—to announce a "Clearance Sale". "Everything Goes!" Clearance Sales also mean cut prices or special red tags and you probably have old tags to cut up and scatter and maybe fake a few oversized ones to announce the sale.

Fixtures that aren't out on the selling floor,—drapers, costumers-even T-stands—can add a spot of interest and a change of pace in a display space that is usually inhabited by mannequins. Give the "girls" a week off—let them rest unseen—and show the outfits draped and slickly shaped on the simple fixtures. With a little imagination you can fashion your own "head" to top the hanger on the draper. Some ideas are provided in other chapters in this book.

Cleaning supplies; mops, pails, brooms and such are also sure signs of a sale in progress. There really is so much just laying around inside the store—you just have to look for them like: hem-markers, steamers, ironing boards and steam irons, your own tool chest and the tools of the trade—unused cash registers—discarded dress forms and all the bits and pieces of antique mannequins.

Out in the street—besides twigs and branches, there are barrier and traffic signs—detour signs—"curves ahead"—stop and go signs—street and road signs—manhole covers—mail-boxes—and more. Some you can get from the local traffic people—some from the Police Department—The Post Office—City Hall. Just approach them and ask them. Don't overlook the mangled pieces of metal—fallen exhaust pipes—unusual "junk"—salvagable salvage—park benches and litter baskets. Bring the outside inside so that those on the outside can be comfortable looking inside.

HENRI BENDEL, West 57th Street, New York City
Window Design: Danuta Ryder

TELLO'S, Cambridge, MA
Display Director: Kathy Shing

B. ALTMAN, Fifth Avenue, New York City
Window Manager: Andrew Druschilowsky
Window Design: David Milutin

Every receiving or shipping department has rolls of lovely beige wrapping paper—crisp, clean and just waiting to be crumpled into a textured background reminiscent of rough mountain terrain or just a neutral colored surface rich with highlights and shadows. You can even save wrappings— the plain brown wrappings and the string that was used, to reuse in your own abstract setting. The "wrapping" suggests a delivery—that something new has arrived and has just been, or is about to be revealed for the first time. The wrapping paper says "Import"—"Just Arrived"— "First Shipment Of"—"Opening Statement"—"For Your Eyes Only".

The cardboard cartons are out there too—under the packing table. They can be stacked neat and orderly, as illustrated on the right, into a series of platforms and plateaus to show small objects at different levels. Cartons tossed helter-skelter through a display area suggest immediacy—a new delivery just pouring in with new, unopened and as yet unseen merchandise. Larger cartons can be used to hold mannequins—either to serve as elevations or as seats. A mannequin can also be half hidden inside the carton. Imagine a row of cartons with only the upper portions of the mannequins showing—and showing off sweaters or blouses or tops. The cartons are neutral in color—they come in a wide variety of sizes and shapes— they are expendable and some even come into your store without your having to pay for them.

GUMPS, San Francisco, CA
Display Director: Robert Mahoney, S.V.M.

B. ALTMAN, Fifth Avenue, New York City
Window Manager: Andrew Druschilowsky
Window Design: David Milutin

RIACHUELO, Sao Paulo, Brazil
Designer: Rommel Rocha

H.A.&E. Smith Ltd., Hamilton, Bermuda
Visual Merchandising Director: Wm. H. Collieson

BLOOMINGDALE'S, New York City
Creative Director: Colin Birch, V.P.

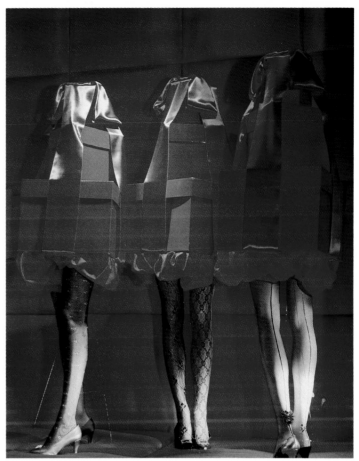

MACY'S, Herald Square, New York City
Window Manager: Linda Fargo

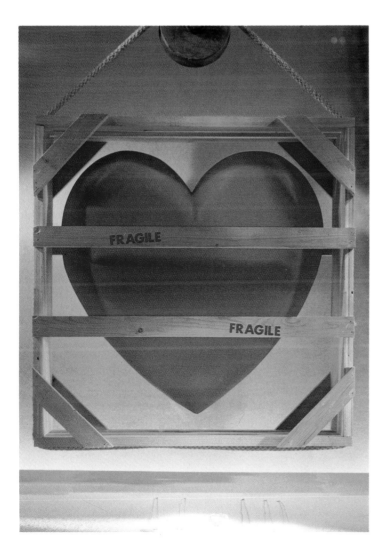

Extra special merchandise—fragile merchandise—or merchandise from far off exotic places, comes packed in raw wood crates. The crates say "imported"—"just arrived"—"handle with care". Inside the crate can be "treasures"—"Fine Art"—"Masterworks". Break open a crate or two to reveal the special merchandise or stack them up into risers, platforms or seats. Stencil your own messages on the wooden slats to indicate the designer or place of origin. The mini-crate with the heart, used in Tiffany's window makes a most unique Valentine display, but the mini-crate could just as easily "contain" some imported leather goods or fashion accessories or precious perfumes. If you have the time, the inclination and the talent, tear the crate apart and put together your own "sculptured" fantasies that are sure to be eye-openers and shopper-stoppers. Store boxes and bags (see next page) are great for an occasional window outing to proclaim a sale or a special event. The boxes make "steps" to show groups of fashion coordinates or accessories on assorted levels,—a natural for shoes and handbags. Not every store has hat boxes but what fun they can be. Stack them into columns that are "classic" with a difference, or convert them into the upper half of a mannequin to show off hosiery or shoes below. Use your imagination—be a little "wild and crazy" —as long as it goes with your store's fashion image.

TIFFANY'S, Fifth Avenue, New York City
Window Design: Gene Moore

13

IN-WEAR MATINIQUE, Washington, DC
Design: **Prop-John Kiser**

OLIVER GRANT, Herald Square, New York City
Window Design: **James Holley**

HARRODS, London, England
Visual Merchandising Director: **John Mac Ketrick**

Your bag is your best calling card. It has your name on it—
your look—your fashion statement. Fill 'em—stack 'em
and pack 'em for Sales and Holiday giving or use them to
pattern a bare back wall.

KENZO, Madison Avenue, New York City

BLOOMINGDALE'S, New York City
V.P. Visual Merchandising: Colin Birch

They're out there—bare, blossomless, colorless, but full of movement and line design, just waiting to be used. Don't chop down a live tree when there are so many "wasted" limbs about that can be used almost anytime of the year. For Spring, add your own "buds"—tissue paper ascatter that is blown on to glue covered branches, or tie on some silk roses or plastic petals—in the right color to suit the merchandise being shown. You only need "suggest" the tree, so a branch or two coming in from one side or the other, or dipping down from the top of the proscenium will get the idea across. For Fall, all it takes are a few russet or golden leaves still hanging on the bare branch. An owl sitting on the naked twig says "Fall" too. If you can get your merchandise to "blow in the wind" (as in the Barney's window) there is no question as to what the setting is all about. For Winter or the Christmas holidays, spray the twigs and branches a shiny white and let them glisten with diamond dust snow. You can add icicles or ornaments, depending upon what you are trying to say. Using ribbon wrapped trunks (Woodward & Lothrop) is another way to go—no matter what the season or the holiday. The natural material can be enhanced by good and effective lighting. The shadows of the intertwining twigs and branches on the back wall suggest a forest or woods beyond. They add depth and dimension to an otherwise flat back wall.

For a surrealistic touch, try a head wrapped in burlap with a twiggy "wig" to top it off. Turn a dress form into a "scarecrow" for showing off Fall suits by having branches extend down through the sleeves and up through the neck—to be capped with the hat of the season.

Talk to the tree pruners, the gardeners, the landscapers in town, and ask them to save their "cuttings" for you. The twigs and branches won't age, fade or wear out, but will be there to serve you through the calendar.

BARNEY'S, Chelsea, New York City
Creative Director: Simon Doonan

"I'M GOIN' WHERE THE SUN KEEPS SHININ' THROUGH THE POURIN' RAIN... GOIN' WHERE THE WEATHER SUITS MY CLOTHES..." OUTERWEAR BY C'EST SIMONE.
INSPIRATION BY "MIDNIGHT COWBOY"

ON 5

GARFINKEL'S, Washington, DC
V.M. Director: R.J. Lester
Window Coordinator: Michael Knicely/Pat Flowers

WOODWARD & LOTHROP, Washington, DC
Div. V.P. Visual Merchandising: Jack Dorner
Washington V.M. Director: Jan Suit

FRED THE FURRIER, Fifth Avenue, New York City
Window Designer: Michael Landry

M.G.A., Beverly Hills, California
Window Designer: Chris Jonic

MONDI, Palm Beach, Florida
Window Designer: Cholsu Kim

BERGDORF GOODMAN, New York City
Director of Design: Angela Patterson, V.P.

You don't have to "steal" what you only have to ask for and borrow. Out in the street, there is all that construction and disruption that makes great window settings for Urban Fashions. The Power and Light Company—the Telephone Company—the road pavers and the salvage savers are all there to be your sources of supply for the everyday "props" that surround us in our daily outings into the street. Look around you and you'll be amazed at just how much is "left" out in the street that is not trash, but is begging to be given a new use. An excellent example is the "ash can art" of the Mondi window, where the refuse takes on a new life as sculpture, and the yellow coat of paint on the exhausted exhaust pipe and mangled mesh become visual assets in selling the yellow separates.

Battered—bruised—beat up bits and pieces, but they still have life, animation and humor to spare in display settings. On the next few pages you will find some amusing attention getting displays that depend upon mannequins who are past their prime for creating realistic fashion images, but are only beginning to come into their own as props. Wrap or strap them with fabric. Paint them or decorate them. Mummify them or let them push forward through jersey covered hoops to make body statements. Let the legs do the walking. Let the hands hold and feet be shoe-shod. Every bit and piece can work, and all it takes usually, is a spray can and a big dollop of imagination well seasoned with humor.

MACY'S, Herald Square, New York City
Window Manager: Linda Fargo

SONIA RYKIEL, Madison Avenue, New York City
Window Designer: Marc Manigualt

MARIO VALENTINO, Fifth Avenue, New York City

MACY'S, Herald Square, New York City
Window Manager: Linda Fargo

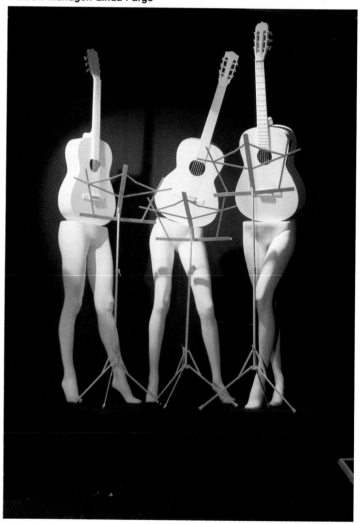

GLORIA PRET A PORTER, Montreal, Quebec, Canada
Decors: Yves Guilbeault   *Photo:* Andre Doyon

ANDRE OLIVER, New York City
Visuals Sitarski/Heneks

2
Furniture

Fortunate is the displayperson whose store has a furniture department as well as a home furnishings or home fashions area rich in accessories for the home. The Furniture department is a gold mine of display props from the hundreds of styles, periods and types of chairs—some illustrated in this chapter—to bigger and more weighty, window-filling props. On the opposite page: a brass bedstead and headboard becomes an enclosed arena for a dress-up, lingerie encounter. Headboards can be a decorative frame to mount on back walls and from which to sweep yards of fabrics—or bedsheets or swag coverlets. Mattresses can in their uncovered, exposed look be an amusing way to show lounging mannequins or to retell the story of The Princess and the Pea; the Princess dressed in her formal best—or in furs—and reclining atop a pile of mattresses. "Fit for a Princess". Along with mattresses go pillows: throw—toss—bed and floor pillows. Create a Turkish harem for maidens in lacy lingerie to loll about in—or let the pillow "fight" it out for a fun, attention-getting approach to White Sales. What says "warm" and "soft" better than downy pillows and puffy quilts?

But—back to the furniture! There are armoires and cupboards and chests,—drawer units, lowboys and highboys,—chests on chests—wooden creations of various periods and places—super-sophisticated or real rustic—that have drawers to pull out and fill or shelves to line or hangrods to hang up garments on. These units not only provide the show space for the garment they provide the ambience and serve as backgrounds in open back windows.

Wicker and rattan furniture can suggest the tropics or Grandma's side porch—or a sun room in Newport—or a scene out of the 20s or 30s. Patio and outdoor furniture open up new vistas for summery dress-ups and party clothes. The colorful PVC kind can be fun—the wrought iron is quite elegant.

A row of theater seats from a razed movie house can be the seat at the opera or ballet that is in town (along with some broadsheets and some programs)—or the barn turned to summer stock,—or even a Retro setting with movie stills from the 40s and 50s. The viewer will fill in the rest of the setting—all they need are the seats and a few "hints" or "clues".

Lamps and Torches can light up the scene and maybe the more the merrier—especially when it is NOT a lamp window. Rugs can be laid on the floor to marl off a vignette setting of chair, table and potted palm—or mounted a back wall as an exotic "oriental" tent—just waiting for a shiek—or cleverly suspended in the window it becomes a "flying carpet" leading to untold adventures—to new fashion finds—to sales—"Up, Up and Away". As it flies in mid window it can carry a mannequin in a fur coat—spread out—to be admired at eye-level—or carry "Light as Air" shoes or luggage.

Chairs, tables, desks, benches and chest,—fine mahogany or lowly but lovely pine—Sheraton or Shaker—neo-classic, art deco—Moderne or Memphis—there is a time for all and the place is in the windows or on the ledges.

FILENE'S, Boston, MA
V.P. Visual Merchandising: **Arthur Crispino**
Boston Visual Director: **Richard Gilchrist**

MARSHALL FIELD, Chicago, IL
V.P. Visual Merchandising: Daniel Burnett
V.M. Director: Homer Sharp, S.V.M.

JORDAN MARSH, Boston, MA
V.P. Visual Merchandising: Linda Bramlage

Small, elegant and lightweight are these opera or ballroom chairs, but they more than carry their weight as display props and in creating display settings. In these few examples you see them lined up, stacked up, and floating off into space—one with a mannequin way up off the ground. By their very styling and nature, they suggest an evening out in formal best, or preparation for an evening at home in luxurious lingerie. Usually they are gilt finished, and the slip seats, so easy to remove and recover, are covered in red velvet. They can be used as chairs for mannequins to sit on—or stand on—or lean against. They may also serve as risers or elevations for fashion accessories and light merchandise. It's nice to be able to own a dozen or so of these finely fashioned chairs to use with Bridal and Formalwear promotions, to feature with furs or frilly underthings on Mother's Day, but if you haven't the budget for the investment, your local caterers or country club might allow you to rent some, or even better—borrow them for a credit card and a thank you.

BERGDORF GOODMAN, New York City
Director of Design: Angela Patterson, V.P.

LA LINGERIE, New York City
Window Design: Geoffrey Howell

WOODWARD & LOTHROP, Washington, DC
Div. V.P. Visual Merchandising: Jack Dorner
Washington V.M. Director: Jan Suit

A single chair can represent a whole room. It can suggest a total setting by its styling, its "period", the covering or the intended use. A simple, unadorned, unvarnished rustic chair speaks for country casuals, and traditional classics. The almost Shaker simplicity of the chair in the Woodward & Lothrop display says "tradition", and also serves beautifully as a raised plateau for an arrangement of all important fashion accessories. The light natural, wood folding chair used at Charles Jourdan is cleverly converted to "wear" a knotted sweater over a pinned up shirt, while another shirt hangs down off the seat. The white sandals take advantage of the arm rests and criss-cross reinforcements to show off and be seen.

CHARLES JOURDAN, Trump Tower, New York City
Window Design: Robert and Steven Balavender

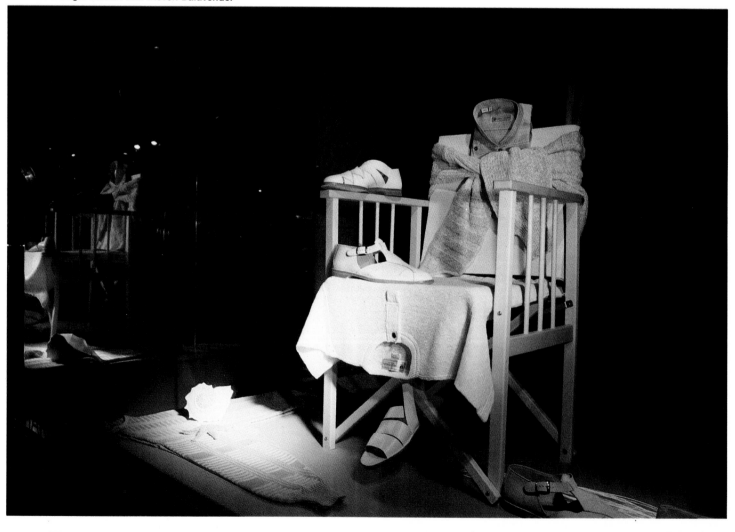

HOLT RENFREW, Vancouver, BC, Canada
Display Director: Bram Bosnack

The heavily carved, dark mahogany arm chair is not an antique, but it certainly suggests the Neo-classic refinement and elegance of mid 18th century England. In the Holt Renfrew vignette setting, (right) the bust on the pedestal and the dark murky oil painting reinforce the image created by the chair. Bentwood chairs, either the old originals or the very new and very inexpensive reproductions are familiar favorites. They are comfortable to sit in, and comforting to be near, because they are so familiar. At Raleigh's they were arranged into an interesting pattern and used as decorative props that also lend balance to the window composition. On the following pages are more "cliche" chairs—chairs that are easily recognizable and provide a sense of place and space—chairs that can tell a story without detailed backgrounds and lots of auxiliary propping. In every instance, they are readily available to the visual merchandiser, and as presented, are as comfortable and effective out on the selling floor—or on a ledge or a platform—as they are in a display window. Since they are all finished "full-round", they can work their wonders in open backed windows as well as in enclosed spaces.

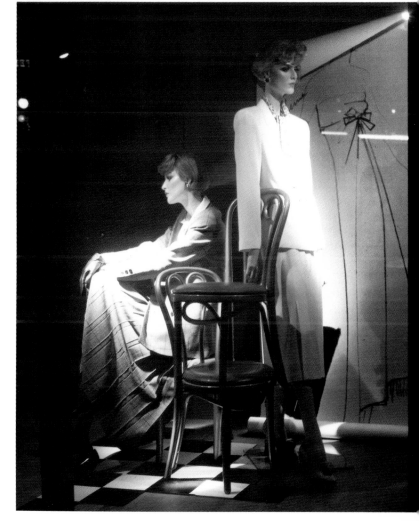

RALEIGH'S, Mazza Gallerie, Bethesda, MD
Director Visual Merchandising: R.J. Lester
Window Coordinator: Michael Knicely/Pat Flowers

FABRIQUE, Rue de Bourdennais, Paris

Easygoing, seagoing casual clothes call for relaxing chairs and here are a variety of sit down stretch out and enjoy the ocean breeze chairs. They go from the canvas covered yachting or director chairs—so easy to color coordinate with the merchandise—to the fabulous ocean liner deck chairs with their lath-stripped foot rests. It can't hurt to add a colorful canvas sun-brella to finish off the setting. The sling chairs on the left have been "re-upholstered" in the featured fabrics that this small Parisian decorating shop was promoting. Below, at the Limited, the two deck chairs "convert" an area into a specialty shop with an island display that sets the scene as well as shows off coordinated merchandise. For a touch of the exotic, the Peacock chair of woven reed and rattan brings back memories of Bette Davis in "The Letter"—of the leafy jungle—of the tropics. In this Ohrbach display, it sets the stage for the vivid tropical floral prints being offered.

In addition to chairs, there are cabinets to open and show merchandise in and on, drawer units that can be stacked to overflowing with coordinates, sofas and couches and bedsteads to provide play space for nightwear. (see Macy's, N.Y. on page 32) If you don't have a furniture department in your store, look to the furniture down the street, or the decorator shop that wants some extra exposure. Your "prop" can be his "ad".

ROSSETTI, Madison Avenue, New York City
Window Design: Chuck Price

THE LIMITED, Madison Avenue, New York City
Visual Presentation Director: Chris Dixon

MACY'S, Herald Square, New York City
Window Manager: Linda Fargo

OHRBACHS, New York City
Director, Visual Merchandising: Jerry Cassese

BURBERRY'S, New York City
Display Director: Michael Steward

MACY'S, Herald Square, New York City
Window Manager: Linda Fargo

N I E D E R M A I E R

2828 N. PAULINA ST. CHICAGO, IL 60657 (312) 528-8123
435 HUDSON ST. NEW YORK, NY 10014 (212) 675-1106

3
Art Supplies/Paints

Fashion is ART—and there is ART in Fashion and in the materials available in the Artist's Supply stores and in the Paint and Wallpaper shops. The materials are ideal for getting across color promotions—new trends—backwards glances to Retro styling—or even further back to past centuries. "Show Your Colors"—"A Call To The Colors"—"Crayola Colors"—"Look to the Rainbow".

Turn a window into an artist's atelier with an easel—some drapes—a lath strip lattice suspended to simulate a "skylight"—lots of paints, brushes and palettes. The Jackson Pollack painted canvas gets an immediate response—and it says ART and it says it in COLOR. We have devoted several of the following pages to frames; picture frames—frames that are truly versatile and adaptive and can be used to highlight in so many ways. Drafting tables and drafting tools belong with architects, designers and engineers and suggest "Construction"—"Well Made"—"Carefully Tailored"—"According to the Plans"—and can become the setting for career-oriented clothes for women and men.

Think Art Supply Store and you think of Art Classes; stools and easels set up—a platform—and on it the model which can be a mannequin in soft chiffon—or elegant sleepwear—or it could just as well be a dressform—elegantly dressed and the stools are "peopled" with mannequins sketching the big fashion news. The same idea could feature a group of budding Michelangelos working at the rotating stands "sculpting" arrangements of shoes, bags and belts. The actual painting and sculpturing classes can become the source for finished "art" to use in a display. Ask for some of the finished students' work and not only will it bring over the students to see their work so publicly "exhibited"—it will also bring out their families and friends. The same goes for all the "week-end artists" who haunt the art supply stores. Those lovely natural wood, collapsible easels/painting kits would make a handsome addition to an outdoor setting for "Watercolor Prints". Wash the walls with blue lights, cover the floor with green grass matting or scatter—set up the easels—open a picnic hamper filled with the right fashion accessories—set a fan blowing out of the viewer's sight line—and what is so rare as a day in the country?

The housepainter can bring a fresh color sense into a display space with his ladders, drop cloths, paint brushes, rollers, paint pans and paint cans. Let him roll some of the featured color on the front glass—leaving just enough undone to show off the new color-coordinated merchandise within. OR—let him or her paint herself into the corner of a window—the floor all shiny wet and gleaming and filled with shoes, belts and bags resting in and dripping out of roller pans and opened paint cans—or skittering over the "wet" floor on paint brushes and rollers. The housepainter could be applying "The First Coat for Spring"—"Coated in Color"—or "Color-Coated". "Enamored with Enamels"—"Stir in Some White"—for "A Great Mix". Drape a paint spattered cloth (of the desired colors) against the front glass—like a tied back, theatrical drape with swag, and use an easel as a sign board to promote an "act" that is "Heading the Bill".

We haven't mentioned all those wonderful rolls of wallpaper that need do nothing more than partially unroll in a window: act as a counterpoint or compliment to a costume—or as a semi-divider in an open back window. The roll of paper by its color, pattern, texture—or period can almost be an entire setting. Maybe all it needs is a single chair of the same period to fill in the vignette.

Here's to the COLOR-CONNECTION.

M.G.A., Beverly Hills, CA
Window Designer: Chris Jonic
Photo: Ted Buel

LOEWE, Rodeo Drive, Los Angeles, CA

Frames! There are hundreds of ways of using frames—large or small frames—to focus the shopper's eye on a collection of coordinates cleverly grouped, or to pick out a mannequin and her costume from a background, or to separate one outfit from another. A frame creates boundaries. It outlines and highlights at the same time. It separates—it organizes—it explains and makes everything seem more important and unique in its glorified isolation. Antique shops may have fabulous frames, ornate, rococo, baroque, Barbizon or neo-classic. The gold leaf finish may be blaringly bright or rubbed to a subtle Florentine finish. The frames can be simple mitred moldings, nailed together, and painted a color that complements or contrasts with the "pictured" merchandise. These simple, unadorned, empty rectangles can, as easily float in open-backed windows or over an island display, as they can set against walls or partitions.

On these two pages and the next one, there are a variety of views of frames in action—as props—as settings—as design highlighters.

COMPLEX DESJARDINS, Montreal, Quebec, Canada
Decors: Yves Guilbeault
Photo: Andre Doyon

FERRAGAMO, New York City
Window Design: David Milutin

36

RALEIGH'S, Mazza Gallerie, Bethesda, MD
Director Visual Merchandising: R.J. Lester

CARSON PIRIE SCOTT, Chicago, IL
V.P. Visual Merchandising: Ron Dascenzo
Director, State St. Store: Susan Stronberg
Window Manager: Michael Williard

A drafting table—a lamp—a pin-up board, and you have a vignette setting for a designer's studio, an atelier, an architect's office or the working space of a design professional. In this setting, we are "Putting Together the Essentials", "Constructing a Wardrobe", "Building a Costume" and putting the "Emphasis on Design" for the "Career Conscious". What about adding the artist's portfolio? The shopper outside immediately recognizes the lady in the window, with the portfolio, as a woman of taste and talent—a lady who knows what to wear, and how to wear it. A portfolio, opened up, with fashion sketches and swatches spilling out, tells another story of "Commercial Art". And, what about the T-squares, the architect's angles and french curves and drawing boards that also identify the professional, and tie in with: "All the Right Angles, (or curves)"—"The Shape of Tomorrow"—"Crisp, Clean and Contemporary"—"Basic Design".

B. ALTMAN, Fifth Avenue, New York City
Window Manager: Andrew Druschilowsky
Window Design: David Milutin

On the next few pages we "add a touch of color" to a promotion. Imagine what you can do with tubes of paint and assorted paint brushes, either on the floor in a pool of colored merchandise, or in the hands of a mannequin adding the final touch to a "painting" on a canvas. The "canvas" can be the background for a still life arrangement in a shadow box or it can be framed and become part of a gallery wall setting. There are the wooden artist's pallettes that go with the tubes of paint and brushes "In the Style of _____", "A Masterpiece of _____" or "Finishing Strokes" for an array of fashion accessories. The easel is another prop that can be more than part of the ambience. It can hold an all important blow-up of a selling ad from a fashion spread or current catalog. The easel can also be a fixture from which a garment can be draped, or on which a costume can be assembled. It not only becomes a focal element—it sends out a message. It says: "The Art of Dressing", "A Composition in Blue (or red or green or whatever)" or "Designed by _____". There are so many trims and displays in the art supply shop or paint store—you just have to do it by the numbers!

KOENING ART EMPORIUM, Milford, CT
Teri Fogler

SAGE ALLEN, Hartford, CT
Director Visual Merchandising: Stephen Delgizzo

ANN TAYLOR, East 57th Street, New York City
Creative Director: Sonny Jaen

BONWIT TELLER, East 57th Street, New York City
V.P. Visual Merchandising: Frank Calese, S.V.M.

ANDRE OLIVER, New York City
Visual Sitarski/Heneks

Splash on the color! Cans of paint can be used as build-ups or as color indicators. "Opened" cans can be used to "pour" out color coordinated fashion accessories like shoes, bags, belts and scarves. There are big bristle brushes and paint rollers to spread the color story smoothly and evenly across a wall or over a floor. There are tarpaulins and drop clothes (Ann Taylor, page 41) that can be used to shroud furniture, or mannequins waiting to be unveiled in the season's newest color scheme. The drop cloths can say, "The First Coat for Spring", "A Cover Up", "Under Wraps" or "Make the Discovery". They can add mystery, suspense and surprise to an otherwise routine display. Sometimes it's what you don't see that sells best! Let's not forget the drawing pads, the colored crayons, the magic markers, the lettering templates that can all do so much in small accessory groupings and that are just right in scale for shadow boxes and display cases. Also small in size, but big on delivering the display message, are the articulated wooden artist's mannequins that everybody loves to pay with—the pose—to set in action. They are great in shadow boxes and up close to fashion accessories and cosmetics. The Lilliputians in a Gulliver sized world can be mighty-mites when it comes to getting the viewer's attention, and even a smile. They can, in larger windows, tie up a mannequin in gold thread—or fit a suit—pin up a rising hemline—tie up ribbons on gift boxes or laces on sneakers and sandals.

So, check out your own art supplies. Don't throw away the old latex paint cans, or the dried out roller you forgot to wash and put away. You can always paint them the color you now want to feature. Save those sheets you've dripped paint on. They might be smashing when you're saying "Splash of Color" or "Paint the Town". Since color is what sells the merchandise, treasure your art supplies and use them in your display set-ups.

BARNEY'S, Chelsea, New York City
Creative Director: **Simon Doonan**

4
Art Gallery/Antiques

You may not have an Art Gallery in your town, but you surely have the "makings" of one. Any store that sells framed graphics or posters can provide you with a "Gallery Wall"—or a vignette setting of a special room—or period—or time. The prints can be anything from Leroy Neiman sports scenes to Old English hunting scenes, from Erte's Art Deco designs to the bold patterns of Mondrian or Leger. Somewhere in all those prints you can find a color compliment—or a setting that is right for the forward fashion trend—or the backward's glance.

The local art schools and colleges can be a mine waiting to be "dug" because "there are displays in them thar halls". Local artists and sculptors can get a "showing" in your windows—and all it will take is a "courtesy of—" card with their names on it. It is a great exposure for new talent, and one never knows where a sale may come from. You might even find that you can make a comfortable and easy-to-live-with arrangement with the local or nearby Art Gallery who will occasionally allow you to feature one of their artists in your better Suits & Dresses windows—or to provide the elegant setting for Formalwear.

Your display area can become an arena in which art contests are held—and "judged" by the passing public. The displayperson must be the referee—the arbiter—and select those pieces of art that best compliment the merchandise being offered. A mural created by grade school children can become a bright, colorful, attention-getting setting for kids' wear—or as a surprise back-up for sharp, strident prints—or a real contrast for black and/or white fashions.

For Easter: try a window filled with large children's drawings of bunnies, chicks, eggs and flowers. For Halloween,—invite the high school kids in—give them an expanse of seamless paper and let them put the "spirits" into your window. Make it a contest! Let different classes, clubs or schools do different windows and watch the publicity—and the viewing public grow.

Back to the professional Galleries:—borrow, or—if desperate rent—the paintings and sculptures. It doesn't take much to create your own "gallery"; a velvet rope and some brass stanchions (or gilded wooden, upright dowels)—a red velvet carpet (or any appropriate color)—a few green palms in brass jardinieres or pottery planters—and the paintings or—"framed outfits" pinned up on the neutral back wall with good, on target light for "The Art of——"

From Antique shops there are those old, familiar Americana items waiting to make their window appearances in "Made in America" promotions or to enhance red, white and blue presentations. Store Anniversaries and Patriotic holidays call for old bicycles (for one or two—or more) and for emptying out Grandmother's Attic; old dress forms with wire baskets, Gingerbread play houses, trunks, rockers, satchels and old quilts. If your Antique Shop hasn't what you need, you might try the local historical societies—the Preservation Home societies—the libraries—the Fire Department—City Hall.

There is a wealth of old, unused, and mostly un-seen "antiques" lurking in basements and attics—and archives. Someone has to snoop them out and offer a credit card for the use. Don't be afraid to ask; all they can say is "no"—but is isn't likely.

BARNEY'S, Chelsea, New York City
Creative Director: Simon Doonan
Window Manager: Stephen Johanknecht

JORDAN MARSH, Boston, MA
V.P. Visual Merchandising: Linda Bramlage
Boston Visual Merchandise Director: Carl Russo

BLOOMINGDALE'S, New York City
V.P. Visual Merchandising: Joe Feczko, S.V.M.

Pedestals, sculptured busts, architectural details—the makings of classic statements. "Classic" is more than Greek and Roman, more than antique. Classic is defined as "having a high quality that is recognized and unquestioned", and "having qualities like simple and harmonious". It is a quality that is often desired, especially in the presentation of up-scaled merchandise. If the name "Liberty of London" wasn't status enough for the bed linens being promoted above, the "classic" elements quickly reassure the shopper outside, that this is "class" merchandise. The vertically channeled pilasters add dignity to the scene that is under the watchful eye of the Greek head on the pedestal. Right: a Roman bust is set akilter as a relief from the exquisite care and precisely line-up merchandise beside it. However, the bust is still "classic" as is the pedestal that seems to support the arrangement.

LORD & TAYLOR, New York City
V.P. Visual Merchandising: **Martha Birmingham**
New York Visual Merchandise Director: **Ken Schleimann**

LORD & TAYLOR, New York City
V.P. Visual Merchandising: **Martha Birmingham**
New York Visual Merchandise Director: **Ken Schleimann**

A classic store presents its classic "image" with these pieces of sculpture. For the window, one doesn't need to have bronze or marble to make the right impression. The dimensional pieces can be plaster casts, and even if a nose is nicked, or a finger is gone, or a base is cracked, the effect can be of "age" and "antiquity". Sometimes a coat of white paint is all it takes, but then again, a fashion color can add a light, sprightly touch to a "classic" setting. The white plaster casts of lips, noses and hands you slavishly copied in art class would be scent-sational for perfumes and cosmetics. Busts and torsos could work for lingerie, sportswear and men's underwear. Some of today's mannequin houses sell fabulous torsos that could be set up on pedestals to create that "classic" look—and still serve as fashion forms. Since sculptures are usually three dimensional, they will work effectively in open windows as well as on the selling floor and on ledges to impart their distinctive qualities to the merchandise on hand.

BONWIT TELLER, East 57th Street, New York City
V.P. Visual Merchandising: **Frank Calese, S.V.M.**
Visual Merchandising Director: **Robin Lauritano**

"Mirror, mirror on the wall—", or off the wall—it has a story to tell. It is revealing—it shows all—and sells all, from any view or angle. Whether it is a framed Venetian fantasy that hangs on a back wall, or a cheval mirror that stands on its own legs and can be tilted and turned, or an architectural pier mirror that is actually part of the wall design, the mirror adds sparkle and shimmer—catches and reflects lights and duplicates what is being presented in the window. The frame or support creates the mood or ambient setting by its styling and its finish. The mirror is an excellent device where the displayperson wants to show both front and back views of a garment, but only use one figure. For bridalwear, the bride can be looking into a full length mirror, while the back of her gown gets a full viewing from the shopper in the street. These props aren't inexpensive, and can be rented or borrowed from antique shops, from auction houses, from better furniture stores, or you could be lucky and find some mirrors in need of love, tender care and repair in second hand shops. Where a less than perfect image or reflection is desired, replace the mirror with a mylar covered panel, or make your own mirrors by inserting mylar in any ornate frames you own or can beg or borrow.

B. ALTMAN, Fifth Avenue, New York City
Window Manager: **Andrew Druschilowsky**
Window Design: **David Milutin**

LORD & TAYLOR, New York City
V.P. Visual Merchandising: **Martha Birmingham**
New York Visual Merchandise Director: **Ken Schleimann**

Miss O by Oscar de la

Screens are always nice to have around and handy for creating a special space. Simple folding screens are excellent for vignette settings—for partially cutting off the view in an open back window—for "suggesting" a back wall where there is none. Out on the selling floor, or up on a ledge, the screen defines and frames off the area. Of course, a Chinese coromandel screen is super elegant, and immediately imparts a class look to whatever is set out in front of it, be it gowns, furs, suits or lingerie. Even here on Madison Avenue, all it seems to take is the "courtesy of" card in lower right corner of the window.

LA LINGERIE, Madison Avenue, New York City
Window Design: **Geoffrey Howell**

I. MAGNIN, Wilshire Boulevard, Los Angeles, CA
Display Director: **Derek Can Syoc**

Let there be light—antique light, chandeliers, candelabras, candle holders and torcheres—ornate, gilded, swirling and ablaze with shimmering crystal prisms. Hang a chandelier and it is Versailles—a ballroom in Newport—a castle in Spain. Leave the chandelier on the floor, or wrapped in net, and it is surrealistic, fantasy, mysterious and a poetic touch for sparkling ball gowns. Doing the unusual or unexpected with a recognizable object is what gets the attention—the ohs! and ahs!—the second look. You don't have to clutter the window to get the message across. A well chosen prop can do it simply, and without distracting from the merchandise.

ELIZABETH ARDEN, New York City
Display Director: **Walter Rummenil**

There are those old, familiar, friendly and always recognizable Americana antiques waiting to make their display appearances in "American Designer" set-ups or "Made in America" events,—to celebrate the annual reappearance of red, white and blue in anything from active sportswear to blue tailored suits with red accessories. Right: Denim is set to travel on a reproduction of a turn-of-the-century bicycle that serves to provide a dash of Americana while holding the three mannequins in a tight, effective composition.

FILENE'S, Boston, MA
V.P. Visual Merchandising: **Arthur Crispino**
Boston Visuals Director: **Stephen Vieser**

BARNEY'S, Chelsea, New York City
Creative Director: **Simon Doonan**

Let's not overlook the everyday "old-timers"—the leather luggage—satchels—portmanteaus—paisley lined Saratoga trunks—and label covered steamer trunks. There are also the gaudy paper wrapped hat boxes of yesteryear. Together or individually they speak of travel—opening vistas—finding new merchandise—of Imports and of stay-at-home, traditional values. The open satchel (Ralph Lauren Polo, p. 54) can hold an array of coordinates and accessories while promising good, old-fashioned "tradition" and "value". If the trunk is large enough, it becomes a chaise lounge upon which a mannequin can stretch out.

ANN TAYLOR, East 57th Street, New York City
Window Design: Perrone/Allen

RALPH LAUREN, POLO, Madison Avenue, New York City
Corp. Dir. of Creative Design: Jeff Walker

MACY'S, San Francisco, CA
V.P. of V.M.: Greg Hribar
Creative Director: Kent Smith
Window Design: Dusty Atkins

CASTNER KNOTT, Nashville, TN
V.M. Director: Elaine Hensley

HENRI BENDEL, West 57th Street, New York City
Window Design: Danuta Ryder

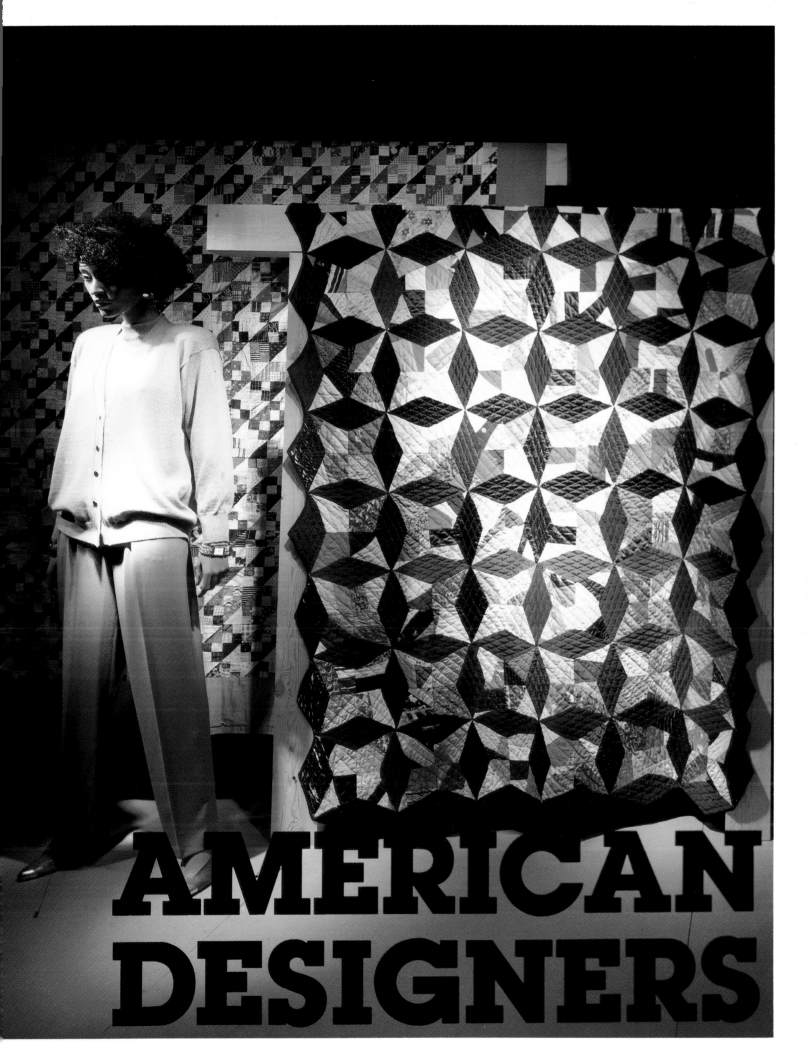

AMERICAN DESIGNERS

Paintings can be found in galleries—in Art studios—in museums—and in public spaces. They add color to the environment and in a window display they can relay the color message across a crowded street. They can enhance the color of the merchandise—make it appear richer—brighter—purer, or they can suggest a palette of colors—the range of colors in which the garments are available.

Right: the rich, hot pink abstraction behind the pink suit seems to glow and send off heat waves that also envelop the mannequin. It helps in that a pink filtered light is washing over the painting and the suit.

B. ALTMAN, Fifth Avenue, New York City
Window Manager: Andrew Druschilowsky
Window Design: David Milutin

Left: Small objects do not always draw viewers—especially when they might be hidden by the people passing by. This painting of a reclining "Odalisque" done in a bold, striking palette of reds, pinks, purples and magentas serves as the "flag"—the attention getter that prepares the viewer for the vivid colored shoes, boots and bags assembled on the pink floor board and backed up by a russet back wall.

I. MILLER, Fifth Avenue, New York City
Window Design: Howard Nevelow

Colonial Presents

GREAT MOMENTS
IN DISPLAY HISTORY

MERLIN INVENTS GLITTER

Colonial

DECORATIVE DISPLAY CO. 160 11TH AVENUE AT 22ND ST., NEW YORK, N.Y. 10011 (212) 255-9620

5
Auto Parts

People are usually fascinated by Automobiles; they are the super status symbols that one can leave out in the driveway for all to see. It is a way of saying—"I Have Arrived". It is who and what the owners may want to be: a sleek, slick, high-speed runabout or an elegant, finely tuned classy chassis. We are definitely a nation of Auto buffs—and buffers.

It is nice to know that the display person doesn't have to necessarily bring the whole car into the window to create a fashion image for the merchandise—or to appeal to the autophiles out front to whom autos are a way of life. Bits and pieces will do; parts are often enough to tell the story. In this chapter we will show some clever uses of tires,—inner tubes—a fender—a door—hub-caps—even half of a 50s pink Cadillac,—but that is only the start.

The Auto Supply Shops have myriad accessories, and since so many are into "wheels"—browse and discover the props: mirrors, directionals, license frames (to carry your message or a designer's name), hood ornaments, auto insignias, fender lights, whipping antennae, bumpers and bumper guards, mats, lambswool covers, etc. "Get Moving"—"Step on it"—"And Away We Go—"—"Off to—"—"Let's Get Going!" Want to "Get Going" in winter outerwear? Why not add some anti-freeze containers; maybe even show the anti-freeze "pouring" into the warm coats and jackets. Need a "Quick Start"? Try a battery and some orange handled jumpers! They're also a sure indication that this is a "Turn-Over" sale. Spark plugs in an accessory case help explain that the small items make an outfit "Go-Go-Go".

Don't overlook the Auto Collector Clubs that appear to be everywhere. Try to get some of the "vintage" autos to feature on the interior—and in the windows if your front glass is removable—for special Anniversary events. You might even approach the "Smiling" auto dealer down the road and get the use of a brand new, shiny, auto—or maybe a Rover or Jeep or Blazer to pack with bright, young sportswear on bright, young looking mannequins. Banana Republic has been using a camouflage jeep as a lay-down displayer in their stores. Maybe you can locate those fabulous, scaled down autos—those exact replicas that are sold at F.A.O. Schwarz. Wouldn't one be great for "young people's" dress-up fashion—for "Back to School"—or as a contrast with adult merchandise?

Have you considered the Auto Racing Societies—for their sporty flags and maybe the use of their loving cups or trophies?

For laydown or background trims—don't overlook the local travel clubs—the AAA and the travel agencies for maps and trip-stripes. They are always a sure indication that Vacation time is near. So,—"Hit the Road"—"Get Going"—"Seasoned Travelers"—and "Traveler's Aids"—the auto—a whole, a half, a fender, a bumper—a gleaming grill—it's a "Great Way to Get There".

PALAIS ROYAL, Houston, TX
V.P. of Visual Merchandising: John P. McCarty
Photo: **Ron Nesch**

CASTNER KNOTT, Nashville, TN
V.M. Director: Elaine Hensley

CARSON PIRIE SCOTT, Chicago, IL
V.P. Visual Merchandising: Ron Dascenzo
Director, State St. Store: Susan Stronberg

FIORUCCI, East 59th Street, New York City
Art Director: Tim Goslin

Tires—black shiny rubber donuts—make a decorative addition to a display either neatly stacked or ring-tossed across the space. They can provide elevations for mannequins—or accessory groupings. Tires suggest the free-spirited, free-wheeling—wild attitude that is great for trendy sportswear and young men's fashions. Old tires—past car bearing—needn't languish in old, back lots. The "baldies" can grow a coat of color and become bright circular "frames" to highlight a particular garment—or just pile up for ambiance. The sleek inner tubes can also add to the overall fun feeling; they can recall those days of our youth when they were our backyard "swings"—or kept us afloat as we skinny-dipped in the local pond. Mirror bright hub-caps can polka-dot a display area with sparkle and pizzaz. They can be punctuation points that direct the viewer to where the action is—and the merchandise is being featured. It is cliche—and sexist—but it is for young men's jeans and sportswear—for teen-agers—"with wheels" and on the go. But why not let the girls go out and "burn some rubber" too. It is a way of life! Some of the new wheel guards are "works of art" and not only bespeak of autos,—they can cast fascinating shadows onto low lit walls and create interesting patterns and intermingled designs.

STEVEN E., Great Neck, NY
Window Design: Mindy Greenberg

BIGSBY & KROTHERS, Chicago, IL
Director of Visual Merchandising: Michael Kelley

I. MILLER, Fifth Avenue, New York City
Window Design: Howard Nevelow

I. MILLER, Fifth Avenue, New York City
Window Design: Howard Nevelow

GOLDI'S, Woodfield Mall, Schaumberg, IL
Designers: **Kubala-Washatko**
Photo: **Mark Heffron**

For total display impact, the front end of a 50s Pink Cadillac appears on the selling floor of a very smart accessory shop. In addition to the car, hub-caps are used as a decorative frieze over the collection of mini-T.V. screens. In another new shop, not pictured here,—Take A Taxi—a vintage checkered cab was cut in half with the front end ripping out of one wall while the rear end is seen disappearing into the opposite wall. You don't have to bring the whole or even half an auto into the window or display space to make a fashion statement! Bits and pieces—parts—doors—fenders—hoods—even just the seats will work. Palais Royal (page 58) gets their Beverly Hills promotion off and rolling with a single door and an unattached tire. The shoppers can and will fill in the missing parts. The "Jalopy" brings back memories of "wild youth" while autos of the 40s and 50s provide settings for Retro fashions. You can get the message across with a suspended windshield—and maybe a fancy grille. The back end of a car—open to the public—can be stacked with luggage—or a lay-down of traveling clothes. While the trunk is open, get out the jacks for some super elevations for special fashion accessories.

SANDY SKOGLUND

Sock Situation

6
Appliances

Who could imagine being turned on by a refrigerator or a stove? Those are things you turn on to get things cold or hot. They are also props for window and ledge displays to promote new seasons—to keep "Something's on Ice"—or to "Take the Chill Out Of—"—to "Heating Things Up"—or "Cool-Calm and Collected". Those large warehouse stores run by the people who insist upon being their own TV spokespersons—who smile at you and promise you the lowest price—well, they might be just the ones to "make you a deal"—and lend you some of their plug-in products to perk up a window. On the following pages we see only the tip of the appliance iceberg; the refrigerators thrown open—the fans blowing—the TV sets flickering— the stoves simmering,—but what about the smaller appliances?

There are the ones that line the kitchen counters—are attached to the walls or crammed into cabinets that also have "lines" to speak. Clocks—all types, shapes and sizes proclaim "Timely" fashion trends and "Of the Minute" colors—"From This Moment On" looks. Coffee Makers—brewers and perkers and drippers could mean something to career clothed couples on the run—"A quick-pick-me-up" for Brown promotions that go from dark brown to cafe au lait. They can set the scene for the "Coffee Break" in the office—or for promotions that are "Perking Up". "The Coffee-ier Coffee"—"The Better Blend"—"Freshly Brewed in the Season's Newest Color" or "Coffee—the Instant In-Color".

Mixers and blenders lined up and overflowing with small fashion accessories: the shoes, belts, bags and scarves that "Mix With—" or "Blend in—"to the newest looks. These could work wonderfully well in shadow boxes or in limited sized cases—"Whipping Up Some Costume Toppers". "In A Spin Over—". A line of steam irons across a window will say something about the way the merchandise holds up. What can you do with a Can Opener? Try opening a "can" and letting the colored accessories spill out into a lay-down arrangement. Toasters and Table ovens can "Pop Up" with all sorts of beige to brown items—or even open up—as the toaster oven—to reveal a warming group of "Toasty & Tasty" accessories. How about something on the Griddle—or Waffle Iron—something that says "Hot Off the Griddle" or "Sizzling Hot".

For Clearance Sales: bring out the vacuum cleaners—the standing ones,—the fat, rolling around ones—with nozzles and yards of cord. Animate them—give them some action as they swoop through the window sucking up the values. "The Big Sweep"—"Watch Things Disappear"—"The Big Clean-Up of Values".

We do touch on the outdoor grills and barbeque appliances but there are more things that can set the outdoor setting—and they also work indoors. There are the radios that ask to be carried out to the beach—or to the picnic—or the ones with clocks that say "Time to Rise and Shine". The HiFi and stereo equipment belong indoors for stay-at-home, laze-at-home, lounge wear.

Back to the big ones: the gleaming white behemoths. Just think of the fun cotton and bright colored sportswear promotions you could prop with washers and driers. Either let the coordinates or accessories appear in the glassed-in frame, or open the washer and/or dryer and let them come out the top or stack up on the pull-down lid. "Easy to Care For"—"Wash & Dry Duos"—"Set It at Cool"—"Quick Drying"—"The Color is In".

Of course, don't overlook the many great possibilities in the old time appliances: the tin tubs and mangling mangles,—the wood burning stoves and the Franklin stoves for wintry settings—the ancient ice-box with the dripping pan beneath—the whisks and beaters that predated vacuum cleaners and sweepers. They say "Anniversary" and "Americana" in a loving, nostalgic manner.

BARNEY'S, Chelsea, New York City
Creative Director: Simon Doonan

RENEGADE, Galleria, Fort Lauderdale, FL
Window Design: Brad Toth

Just plug in a display! You can swing open a refrigerator door and it's an invitation to "Cool off"—with fashions you've been "Keeping on ice". Just imagine how well accessories could be arranged on the shelves and in the extended crisper bins—to say nothing of finding "ice"—real or fake—in a freezer compartment. What about a kitchen full of appliances (Barney's on page 64)—stove, oven, fridge—the kitchen sink—all to "Heat Things Up" or to sell "Simmering Fashions"—as well as supply scale and bulk to a window presentation? Above: a sale was in full swing and it was time to "Clean Up" with brightly colored carpet sweepers—picking up colored sawdust while the balance of the window was a maze of swinging electrical wires—also in matching colors. The color-keyed masks on the black, soft-sculptured mannequins were a nice added attraction. We go out-of-doors with appliances like gas grills and barbeque equipment—and all the Summer pleasures they portend—and the wide range of merchandise they can assist in promoting. "Look what's cooking"—"Right off the grill"—"Turned to perfection"—"When the living is easy".

M.G.A., Beverly Hills, CA
Window Designer: Chris Jonic

F. BODNER, Bal Harbour, Miami, FL
Window Design: F. Bodner

LORD & TAYLOR, New York City
V.P. Visual Merchandising: Martha Birmingham
New York Visual Merchandise Director: Ken Schleimann

BLOOMINGDALE'S, New York City
V.P. of V.M.: Colin Birch

And—if its hot, try cooling off with fans; floor fans—
window fans—and even the Casablanca-styled ceiling fans.
They will all put some animation in your display—get some
gentle fabrics stirring—create easy breezes that catch
streamers, ribbons or pennants and set them rippling. Line
them up for the effect, and remember,—the little ones nod
from side to side and can be quite amusing while some of
the bigger ones, in their chromed cages, can add some shine
and sparkle. The clothes lines make nice additions,
especially in an open back window. It gives the fan's
current something to react against.

You can't get away from them so why not bring the
telephones into the window—but bring along yards and
yards of coiled cords to stretch across the display space. It's
a great device for "Spreading the News"—or to get the
message across. Call the greater Bell Telephone company or
any of their hundreds of subsidiaries and they should be
pleased for the exposure of their different styles,—from
"executive suite" specials for career conscious dressing to
"Mickey Mouse" and his friends for Junior events.

WITHOUT LIMITS, New York City
Window Design: David Bradescu

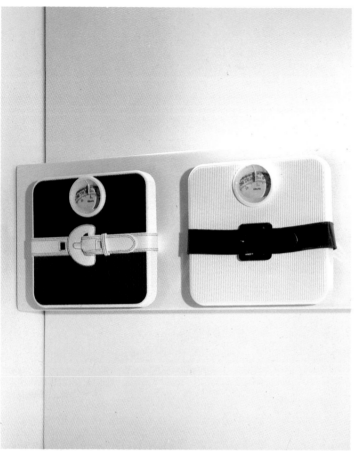

MACY'S, Herald Square, New York City
Window Manager: Linda Fargo

BERGDORF GOODMAN, New York City
Director of Design: Angela Patterson, V.P.

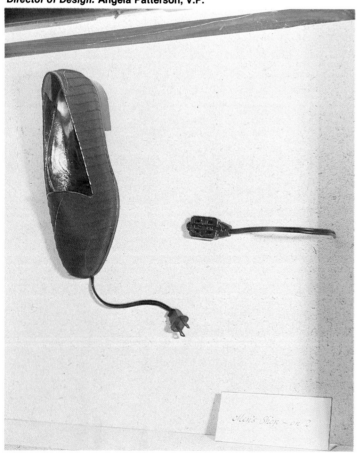

TIME FO

KAUFMANN'S, Pittsburgh, PA
V.P. of Visual Merchandising: David Knouse
Downtown V.M. Director: Anthony Lucas

R THE BODY SUIT

Everybody talks about it and most people dread the moment of truth, but scales—bathroom scales can tip in big when it combines with small, lightweight items that are heavy in fashion. "Tip the scale in favor of"—"Heavy-weights" or "Lightweights". Not only are they effective for fashion accessories like belts—where the weight shows—and shoes, but they can tell a convincing story for luggage. The small kitchen scales shouldn't be overlooked when planning shadow boxes or cases.

Clocks—all types—shapes—sizes—styles—and faces are perfect for "Timely" displays. So many are battery operated—and lightweight—that making a clock mask to fit over the mannequin's face should be quite simple. But do get them started and ticking; people will stop and check out the time as well as the merchandise. "Time marches on!"

THE LIMITED, Madison Avenue, New York City
Director Visual Presentation: Janet Mansour

A group of mannequins are surrounded by T.V. sets on the lowest level of The Limited and the sets play with a Busby Berkley precision that is graphically exciting and satisfying. A few suspended lightweight sets set the look for the Red Bag trendy shop at Robinson's and the coiled wires come in for action and interest. The abstracts at Gimbels lost their heads to TV but the personal size TV sets work so much better and are so much more effective for the merchandise being offered—and for the clients they are being offered to. It is easy to see what's on one's mind when you can see it on a screen—and in color.

GARFINKEL'S, Washington, DC
V.M. Director: R.J. Lester

ROBINSON'S, Horton Plaza, San Diego, CA
V.M. Director: Jack Hruska, V.P.

GIMBELS, New York City
V.M. Director: Bernie Hauserman, V.P.
Window Design: Nora Peer

No Junior promotion—or for that matter—no Designer promotion seems to be able to do without a TV set—a VCR attachment—and often it is the more the merrier. Everybody watches TV screens and oddly enough it is more than the "couch potatoes" who watch. People will stop and watch almost anything on a TV screen—in a window or on the selling floor. Top designers replay tapes of their runway shows or show an expanded line—or introduce their new perfumes or cosmetics—and shoppers line up to watch commercials they can sit down and see at home. For the Juniors it can also be a line presentation or music videos that seem to work—even when one can't hear the throbbing beat.

7
Grocery and Produce

The local grocery—the gourmet shop—the fast food operation—the supermarket and the hypermarket—the outdoor market—the indoor market and the farmer's market,—they all abound in the bounties of nature and are ready, willing and able to add their colors and textures to display set-ups. In this chapter we will show the fruits and vegetables right off the vine—off the food stands,—the canned foods—the burlap bagged coffees, rices and beans of many colors—the bottled condiments—the jars of jams and jellies—the salamis and spices—and in passing a mention of big brown paper bags and shiny shopping carts that can be loaded with coordinated merchandise—or proclaim a sale where you "Take It Away".

Think of cereal boxes that suggest the "Pop, Snap and Sparkle" of a new outfit or trendy sportswear—or the rich beiges and browns of the merchandise pouring out of an opened box into a cereal bowl already overfilled with small accessories. What is more fitting than "Oatmeal"—regular or quick cooking—for the pretty off-white fabrics and pale beige leathers? From the cereals to the breads and rolls that may go hard in a window but never stale when promoting the wheat tones—the rye-beiges and pumpernickel browns. They are always "Fresh"—"Oven Baked"—"Bisquit Beige"—"Just Browned"—"Good, Old Fashioned Flavor-ites". The cakes, cookies and pies are also display props—unless you have mice who "do" the windows. Oreos and Mallomars—in their recognizable boxes—are spokes-objects for chocolate browns and creamy whites. They too are "Old Fashioned Favorites". Donuts can tell the "Whole Fashion Story" and what is more American—more red, white and blue than Mom's Apple Pie—steaming up a window with its fresh baked goodness. You could spray or coat the pie with clear lacquer or shellac for that nice, glazed look.

For Import Promotions; get them where they can taste it! Visit the local ethnic groceries or the fancy import gourmet shops for cans of olive oil from Italy, Greece, Spain or Portugal,—giant jars or vats of black or green olives—the marvelous, odoriferous cheeses of Italy, Switzerland, Denmark—the giant wheels stamped with the place of origin, or the blimp-like provolones wrapped in twine,—the bright red and gold Edam cheeses from Holland—English Cheddar—fancy camemberts from France. Many cheeses do not need to be kept on ice or refrigerated while still in their colorful, protective coatings—and that is what we want to see—and show. It is surprising how effective salamis, sausages and wursts can be in a display—and how distinctive—in an Import Fair.

Supermarkets, in addition, carry cleaning supplies, soaps and detergents—kitchen appliances and devices—candies and chocolates and nuts by the pound or the bag—shelled or unshelled. So, go visit one soon just to make up a shopping list for future displays. It's always a good idea to see what is in season to promote what you have for the season.

WEISFIELD'S, Seattle, WA
Display Manager: Sharon Whittlesy
Visual Artist: Chuck Ratcliffe

ALEXANDER'S, Lexington Avenue, New York City
V.M. Director: Sal Marra

FIORUCCI, East 59th Street, New York City
Art Director: Tim Goslin

Food—Glorious FOOD. Edible and incredible—taste tempting hors d'oeuvres that are sure to please the palette. The local grocery and supermarkets are abounding with "specials" that not only lend their unique qualities to the display set-up,—they can later be eaten at leisure. It is a natural to tie in Coca Cola—in cans, bottles or dispensing machines—with Coca Cola clothes, but the Coke or Pepsi drinks also say "vacation"—"beach"—"picnic"—the "pause that refreshes"—and time for fun and to frolic. They reiterate the red, white and blue fashion promotions and are as "All American" as the sportswear or denims they accompany. You may not even have to rush down to the supermarket for the cans,—they are probably stacked up out in the employees' cafeteria—or at the soda machine where you can borrow them for a week or two of window or ledge exposure. Sprite is lemon/lime and could identify with those colors in a promotion just a Mountain Dew is rich in Orange.

Canned foods not only have a long shelf life,—they can also have a short but effective life in display. Campbell's Tomato soup cans were familiar and famous before Andy Warhol blew them up into print prominence. Shelves filled with the family favorite red and white cans—tier upon tier—says "RED"—simply and dramatically. The Weisfeld's "Souper-Sale" is an excellent take-off on the Campbell's cans used with great style and flair to sell better jewelry. It isn't difficult to "package" your own product—to sell it. Since Grocery shopping is becoming so much a part of our social life—and reading labels is a way-of-life,—this is where life is actually lived. Bring that "life" into the window and "Check Out" in style and fashion. Big brown kraft paper bags and chromed push carts make excellent accessories for all that food, packaged goods and small fashion accessories to tumble out of.

Eggs—fragile but fabulous—especially at Easter time when they can be super elegant as shown, right, in Tiffany's window. Or, they can be fun—brightly colored and rolling around on grass covered window floors—stored in straw baskets—or piled up in display cases. Handle with care,—blow them out if you can or boil them hard. Remember, though high in cholesterol they rate even higher in "seasonal recognition"—and they are cheaper by the dozen.

TIFFANY'S, Fifth Avenue, New York City
Window Design: Gene Moore

BERGDORF GOODMAN, Fifth Avenue, New York City
Director of Design: Angela Patterson, V.P.

BONWIT TELLER, East 57th Street, New York City
V.P. Visual Merchandising: Frank Calese, S.V.M.

Fresh produce;—fruit that adds color and flavor to black and white or color-filled patterns. For a week or two in the window—the oranges, lemons and limes will keep their citrus-y sparkle, whether tumbled about or carefully spaced out on a sand-covered floor. Mix them and match them—group them or scatter them—blend them or balance them. You can even try juggling them for a laugh. A refreshing addition to a spring-summer display.

KAUFMANN'S, Pittsburgh, PA
V.M. Director: David Knouse, V.P.
Downtown Visual Director: Anthony Lucas
Downtown V.M. Manager: Jack Neuser

CINDI'S, Syosset, NY
Window Design: **Mindy Greenberg**

What would Fall or Halloween be without pumpkins? They can be more than the traditional grinning jack-o-lanterns; they can finish off "straw stuffed scarecrows" that wear featured outfits—can replace the familiar head of a mannequin—top off a topless dress or costume—or as shown on the opposite page,—a gilded pumpkin wearing a coolie hat can add an exotic semblance to garments skewered on wooden dowels. All it takes is a dash of imagination and a splash of daring. More tropical fruits appear on page 83 and turn knitten cotton sweaters into "Pineapple Shakes". The hula skirts are as Hawaiian as the pineapples—they add to the atmosphere and also unify the mannequins putting the emphasis on top—on the juicy, pale yellow white tops washed in golden light.

JONES OF LONDON, Beverly Hills, L.A., CA

In addition to cans of food and boxes of detergents—soaps and cereals, there are the see-through bottles on the shelves that can add to your display scene. In addition to olives, shown below, there are red spaghetti sauces and creamy Parmesan cheeses to sprinkle on Italian Imports,—marracino cherries to top off a "strawberry" or vanilla" sundae of summer fashions—and so much more. There are also burlap bags filled with beans of many colors—pearly white rice and brown rice—rich aromatic coffee beans—and spices like brilliant paprika or neutral pepper. Some examples are shown on the next page.

Before you leave the spice and condiment section—consider the possibilities and copy tie-ins with Mustard ("Put some Spice in your wardrobe")—Catsup ("Redder than Red")—Mayonnaise ("The Perfect Blend") or Black olives for deep, richer, flavorful blacks. They can be "Flavorful Additions" to the displays.

LA LINGERIE, Madison Avenue, New York City
Window Design: Geoffrey Howell

BLOOMINGDALE'S, New York City
Creative Director: Colin Birch
Window Design: Robin Lauritano

UNGARO, Madison Avenue, New York City
Window Design: Marc Manigault

HENRI BENDEL, West 57th Street, New York City
Window Design: Danuta Ryder

LORD & TAYLOR, New York City
New York Visual Merchandise Director: Ken Schleimann

PINEAPPLE

8
Garden Supplies /Nurseries

The flowers that bloom in the spring tra-la—are tulips, daffodils and long sprays of furry, pussy willows. The live, blossoming plant of pink, white or cerise azaleas are also on the Fashion Calendar to brighten up navy suits and gray Spring outfits. Now is the time to get rid of the tired, faded, and fake-as-fake-can be sprays of forsythia that you store away each year—only to resurrect as a life-less acknowledgment to a season which is all about birth and rebirth.

There is a whole vocabulary of floweres and plants available to the interested and imaginative display person—just waiting to be used in new "sentences"—but always understandable to the shoppers and the window viewers. Magnolias bespeak "The Old South"—gracious living—elegance and refinement. The Cactus plants in their infinite variety and sizes—with or without their brilliant, unexpected, exotic blossoms are: desert, the West—leather, buckskin and denims—boots and saddle-bags—turquoise and silver jewelry. The Cacti are there to introduce the beige, sand tones—the off-white of Georgia O'Keefe skulls and bones—or to contrast with the vibrant sunset colors that shimmer in the Painted Desert.

Lilys of the Valley are the May flowers—fragile, delicate and aromatic. Asters and Mums recall Fall—the football games when racoon coats were "hot diggity dawg"—and the rich palette of harvest colors: golds, ochers, russets and garnets. Why use old "phonies" when fresh ones are available—to borrow or to buy—at the Nurseries or Garden Supply Houses? Have you considered turning over your store windows—for Spring—to the local garden clubs in town? Make it a competition—let the clubs or organizations compete with each other for the best presentation of blooming plants—or floral arrangements—within the perimeters set by yourself. The same can be done with ledges inside the store. Not only will it bring in free publicity from the media,—it will also bring in the friends and neighbors of the participants—the members of the clubs—and all the curious who heard or read about the event. If your community is rich in Landscape Designers—maybe they would like to get into the act—for publicity?

Aside from the plants—the shrubs—the bushes—the trees either in oversized clay pots or with their roots wrapped in burlap,—look at all the other "props" that are lying about; the wheelbarrows to fill with fashion accessories or used to "transport" a mannequin,—the hoes, rakes, shovels and such,—the bags of peat moss—the clay pots and the plastic ones,—the weeders and the reapers. What about all those different machines that are used to mow and trim the lawn? The grass cutters, clippers and shapers? All you have to supply is either green grass mats for the floor—or grass scatter—or even inexpensive green indoor-outdoor carpet will do. The b-i-g lawn mowers—the kind you ride around in not only tell a Spring story,—they take up space and volume and add ambiance. "Making the Summer Scene"—"Shift into Summer"—"It's Green-Up Time"—"Spring is Bustin' Out All Over" and Spring has Sprung".

BEYEL'S, Zurich, Switzerland

MACY'S, Herald Square, New York City
Window Manager: Linda Fargo

FILENE'S, Boston, MA
V.P. Visual Merchandising: Arthur Crispino
Boston Visual Director: Richard Gilchrist

B. ALTMAN, Fifth Avenue, New York City
Window Manager: Andrew Druschilowsky
Window Design: David Milutin

Flowers and plants are ambassadors for so many seasons and holidays. They bring official greetings that Spring is on the way (forsythia—pussy willows—daffodils)—that Mother's Day is a week away (pink carnations)—or that Santa and his sleigh will be counting down the days (poincettias). Lush, tropic palm trees and broad leafed plants—even in pots, suggest Southern climes—resort areas—jungles—safaris—places where the sun always shines and it is deliciously warm—relaxed and the clothes and colors are easy going. "Adam and Eve" can appear amidst the camouflage of foliage—with not a fig leaf or apple tree in sight,—and so can bold, splashy floral prints. In planters, the assorted types of palms can create in the sketchiest of windows; the ambiance of a formal ballroom—an art gallery—or even a hotel lobby in Bermuda. What better—and less expensive-way of welcoming Spring than windows filled with live, blooming plants supplied by local nurseries—or that the store can buy and then present to hospitals, nursing homes, or even donate to town squares or gardens. A good floral display doesn't die or wilt,—its memory lingers on even after the petals fall, but—please—not in the window!

Garden hoses add a swirl of interest to Spring windows as they coil and squiggle their way around the display space—snaring and bringing coordinates and outfits together. They are long and mischievous—seemingly with lives and wills of their own—but they are always interesting. Hoses come in many colors and lengths—if a color coordinated theme is desired. In the semi-realistic setting below, the garden hoses strike a note of realism in a decorative milieu. The ambitious and patient displayperson can "train" the hose to point out special features—to coil up like rubber snakes and serve as elevations for shoes—bags—belts—even garden-scented perfumes and cosmetics. "Unwind in ____"—"Everything is Coming up____"—"The Fashions That Bloom in the Spring". For a humorous approach—think of what one can do with garden hoses and raincoats with or without umbrellas with the addition of some "tinsely" water streaming from the nozzle. Or,—invite your viewers to a "Hose Down" with the season's swimwear—or in ever-loving denims.

UNGARO, Madison Avenue, New York City
Window Design: **Marc Manigault**

M.G.A., Beverly Hills, CA
Window Designer: **Chris Jonic**
Photo: **Ted Buel, Los Angeles**

LINTON'S, Pittsburgh, PA
V.M. Director: **Don Bauman**

Going to pot? Never! The old, clay flower pot is another harbinger of Spring whether left in its natural state or given a strong, fashion-right expression. Here they are worn as bright color accents in a window already brilliant with color and pattern. They do carry through the floral theme. For small fashion accessories; the flower pots—stacked, inverted, toppled over—even broken—can become seasonal elevations that separate groups—or colors—or assemble small objects for easy acceptance. Fill the pot with styrofoam and top it with moss and it is ready to show shoes—to sprout cosmetics—or even bloom with silk roses or overflow with strings of pastel colored beads—bangles —or other "bounties" of Spring. Flower pots come in myriad sizes and shapes—in clay and in brilliant plastics—and there is always the spray can on the shelf.

LA MARCA, East 57th Street, New York City
Window Design: **Marc Manigault**

"Rake up the_____"—"Gather in_____"—"A Sweep of _____"—and all it takes are the rakes—the hoes—the leaf sweepers and gatherers—and the many assorted gardening tools and appliances that line the walls and shelves of the Garden Supply Houses. They "speak" for the merchandise. The tools add the atmosphere while they also lend themselves to merchandising the garments—or supply the mannequins with "action". Sweaters and tops can be stretched across the wooden handles or, as shown, ties, belts and scarves can be draped over them. You can make your own "scarecrow" by lashing a dowel perpendicularly across the rattan leaf rake, just under the sweep of curled prongs. Paste some eyes and a mouth on the triangular "head"—and you've got a fall draper full of style and panache. Pile in the leaves—then sweep some aside to reveal a laydown of accessories and coordinates.

VICTORY SHIRTS, New York City
Window Design: **Bob Kershaw**

LAZARUS, Dayton, OH
Visual Manager: **Kurt Millikin**

HIRSHLEIFER'S, Manhasset, NY
Visuals Sitarski/Heneks

Bushel baskets and fruit crates are often just waiting to be picked up—turned over—and used as platforms—as seats—as plateaus for groups of accessories. Left in their naked, neutral state they are easy blending beiges that are "there" but "disappear" in the scene. Sprayed white, black or a keyed in color, they make a special statement in the setting. They are like the flower pots of Spring—easy to use—to get—and to recognize as a Fall symbol. "Reap the Harvest"—"Bring in the Crop"—or "Come Fill up with ____". From small berry and peach baskets to large apple bushels, they can become the total propping of a shadow box to a window display—to an on-the-floor island display or ledge trim. Again, a lid set into the bushel—then overflowing with fall leaves for a "Harvest of ____" apples, pears, gourds, etc.—that is all it takes. The leafy heads are an extra effective touch. Protect the mannequin's face and make up with saran wrap—then wrap it well with strips of burlap—spray coat with glue and pile on the leaves. The leafy mitt is added on over the hands.

9
General Store

This is the General Store way down in town—down from the "Little House on the Prairie". It is where you can find anything because it is the only store in town. Our General Store of Ideas has ribbons, laces (to trim or to tie), rolls of fabric of every pattern, texture and fiber content,—the dress forms to show off the "ready-mades", feathers to trim more than hats as well as the hats that are to be trimmed. The store also has the umbrellas that shield from sun and from rain as well as needles, threads, skeins of wooly yarns and the big, click-clicking needles you use with them. We have the luggage for short trips or ocean voyages and much more.

If your general store is limited in its stock appeal, here are some other specialized shops you might look into for props:

- Flower shops or Florist Suppliers for real values on ribbons, styrofoam shapes, forms and balls,—spray dyes, covered wired for draping and shaping—floral tapes of many colors. The Neon Sign shop for any of the magic pencil-lines of luminescence in brilliant, eye-straining colors. Neons mean "young", "junior", "trendy" and "fun".

- The Window Blind store for vertical blinds or horizontal blinds with maxi-or mini slats of myriad colors to use as panels of color in open backed windows—to divide run-on windows—to mask or cut down too-tall windows. Or the accordian pleated blinds—or the elegant Austrian Shades—or the mottled, malacca or split bamboo blinds with memories of "The Letter"—the tropics or jungle settings,—or even just the old fashioned roller shade that can be made with almost any length of fabric.

- The Locksmith for locks and keys—for "The Way to Her Heart"—for Valentine's Day—to "Open the Season" or "Release" some new trends. Locks and keys go with yards of chains; nickel plated, steel, brass and even the chains can be swooped through a window or hung down in varying lengths for an unusual "curtain" or proscenium treatment. "Save this—".

- Pet Stores have the doggies that are in the window—but use plush ones instead. They do, however, have the metal grid cages for "tame" animal prints or faux-furs, the beds and comforters for pusses and pooches, the baskets, the traveling cases—the bridles, the collars, the chokers and leashes. Look at them and think what you can do; the mannequin walking an invisible dog off leashes attached to collars suspended from above,—the cat or dog's woven, rattan bed-basket used for "faithful" accessories or shoes resting "cozy and comfy". It can be "Real Friendly". Bird cages—with or without the make-believe birds—hanging or standing, are Spring Symbols. Fill the cage with co-ordinated fashion accessories and set a patient puss of plush just outside waiting for the moment. "Don't Let it Get Away"—"Get the Choice Selection"—"Purr-fect with Navy". Bird Cages come in metal and rattan—in many sizes and finishes. Some are meant for use—some for show. Tired old ones can be revived by a spray can of enamel—and often those tired old ones have been retired to second hand shops and are yours for just a little more than the asking.

Without General-izing, some of the ideas on the next pages come right out of "Notions"—and they do tie up a display in ribbons and bows.

LOEWE, Trump Tower, New York City
Window Design: **Toshi Studio**

CHARLES JOURDAN, Trump Tower, New York City
Window Design: David Bradescu

High flying—for fair or rainy weather—right side up—turned over—inside out—umbrellas are spectacular props for Spring showers—for Summer Summers—and for Fall's windy blasts. They can provide a dash of color—spirited action—excitement to an otherwise staid display. At Loewe, on page 92, the sprightly colored umbrellas shield and gather together under them color stories; presenting three variations by color in a single easy to look at—easy to comprehend display space. Left: carried away in a breeze are colored umbrellas that fly into the viewer's eye and then leads down to the wind-blown fashions below. At Loewe, the umbrellas are turned upside down to catch the downpour of white leather bags in this attractive Spring into Summer display. The umbrella also can be a background in an open back window or provide a bull's eye of color for an outfit. Connections gets down to basics; the wire armatures of the umbrellas create a patterned metal/wood sculptured background in the shallow display space while two traditional big, black nylon covered ones provide contrast for the white sweater against the white wall. Umbrellas are not only available in assorted sizes and colors and patterns—from dainty parasols—to rain umbrellas—to sun-shading, 6' diameter umbrellas—if you don't see what you like, plain white ones can be sprayed or magic-markered to go with special colors or patterns.

LOEWE, Rodeo Drive, Los Angeles, CA

CONNECTIONS, Columbus Avenue, New York City
Director of Visual Presentation: Craig Payt
Assistant: Helena Dietreichs

BLOOMINGDALE'S, Lexington Avenue, New York City
Visual Presentation Director: Joe Feczko, S.V.M., V.P.

HENRI BENDEL, West 57th Street, New York City
Window Design: Danuta Ryder

Ribbons and streamers—by the roll or by the yard—narrow silk strips to wide bands of taffeta—shiny plastic lengths or bold swatchs of cotton canvas; the effects are infinite. Fill a background with bows to emphasize a feminine promotion like lingerie—or Mother's Day, or when bows, with or without buttons, are a fashion note or motif. Let it rain ribbons—bright, bold, strongly colored rivulets that become vertical, semi-see-through curtains that the shopper can see from afar—and that beckons her to come closer for a better view of mannequins emerging from the silky downpour.
Let it rain ribbons for April showers and rainwear—and the umbrellas we just saw. Blue and green cellophane ribbons create "watery" cascades for swimwear and active sportswear.

Right: A dramatic statement against the front glass that could also be painted on—or be stretched black vinyl bands that balance the display and also cut down on the expanse of window.

BERGDORF GOODMAN, New York City
Director of Design: Angela Patterson, V.P.

Fabrics—also by the roll or by the yard—to stretch—pull—shape—drape—wrap—twist and tieback in a display set-up. Great sweeps of natural muslin, available in window proportioned widths of 96'' and 108'' can become backgrounds—can be "ripped" into a tent-like, proscenium opening—or just swaddle mannequins into mummies—and furniture into items of mystery. Stack up the flat folded fabrics holders to provide a seat for a figure while showing off an assortment of go-with patterns and colors for shirts and blouses—or alternate suiting materials.

Fabrics on rolls can unwind into background panels or "window shades" that block the view through into the selling space—or a colorful back-up for the merchandise in front. What says "Jersey" so effectively as the stretch and pull of the fabric itself? Cut a few holes in the fabric that gives—and watch it give new excitement to the display as its "swiss cheese" look makes places for mannequins to step in and out of. Use fabrics for their color—their patterns—their textures,—for what they show and what they can hide. Use sheer fabrics up against the glass for an intimate—semi-hidden effect—as teasers or semi-revealers in the middle of the window or behind the merchandise for contrast or as a color enhancer.

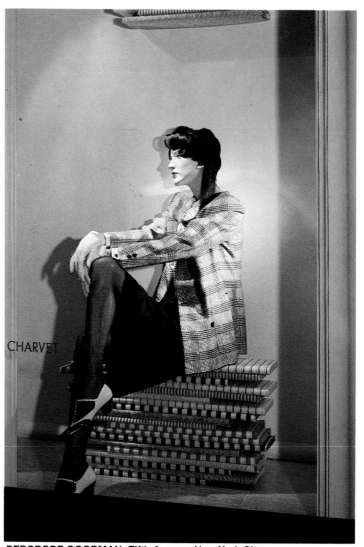

BERGDORF GOODMAN, Fifth Avenue, New York City
Director of Design: **Angela Patterson, V.P.**

HENRI BENDEL, West 57th Street, New York City
Window Design: **Danuta Ryder**

BARNEY'S, Chelsea, New York City
Creative Director: Simon Doonan

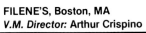

FILENE'S, Boston, MA
V.M. Director: Arthur Crispino

HENRI BENDEL, West 57th Street, New York City
Window Design: Danuta Ryder

LAURA ASHLEY, East 57th Street, New York City
V.M. Director: Barbara Kleber

These are off-color and on-color yarns—and the stories they tell are bright, amusing and have happy sales endings. What says "sweaters" or "knitwear" with more clarity or competence than balls of yarn and knitting needles? Whether the strands are knotted and twisted into one another and formed into Mrs. Haversham hair-dos—messy, mixed up but magical in effect, or carefully wound into tidy balls and neatly arranged as only Grandma would do them,—they can and do go to the head and can turn heads in a sweater sweeps. Balls of yarn in baskets are lovely—color-filled settings for small fashion accessories like "wooly" mittens, gloves and scarves. Add a furry cat and its just like "home".

HENRY LEHR, Madison Avenue, New York City

Packed up and ready to go. For on-the-move fashions—for separates that ask to go-with—to get across the holiday or vacation promotion,—get some luggage into the window—already stuffed with the newest or opened to reveal all the coordinates that will make one outfit into a wardrobe of outfits. If you carry the bags—show your bags, and if you don't carry any in stock—try the luggage store down the street and offer them a viewing of their merchandise in your window along with your travel oriented merchandise—and a "courtesy of ____" card.

MADISON AVE. HABERDASHERY, New York City

10
Hardware

Become a hardware store aficionado; not just the little "hammer and nails" stores—but the big ones that can supply almost anything and everything for the weekend carpenter/builder/handyperson—and the displayperson. In this chaper we will show you some creative uses of ladders, mesh, grids, barrels, pails, rope and twine, all sorts of lighting equipment, brooms and dust pans,—but there is so much more on the shelves and in the big wooden kegs standing on the floor.

The cooking equipment and utensils; the pots and pans—the spatulas, ladles, forks, salad bowls, fry pans, roasters and more and more. "Look What's Cooking"—"Out of the Frying Pan and into Fashion"—"Simmering"—"Keeping Warm"—"Fashion on the Front Burner"—"A serving of—". Imagine what one could do with the small fashion accessories with some of the above: shoes in pots and pans—belts or laced sneakers or shoes in sieves or colanders—or, for that matter,—any Italian promotion highlighted with fashionables mixed with "spaghetti"—in oversized colanders.

When we talk of "oversized"—of big scale, attention-getting pots and pans—you may have need to visit the Restaurant Suppliers for those. Those super-sized, gleaming aluminum beauties can be the setting for your mannequin doing the "Birth of Venus" as she rises up out of one. The coordinates and separates can "boil over" the tops—when some clear glass bubbles are added to the pot. In addition,—the Restaurant Suppliers have the big, beautiful coffee urns that say "Coffee Brown" at a glance. "Brewed to Perfection"—"The Best Taste in the Morning". There are also the rolling carts—the wire and chrome racks and stands—the soup tureens—and the silver domed serving trays that make whatever is showing beneath the tilted dome—"A Feast for the Eye"—"A Gourmet's Delight"—"Especially for You"—"Served on a Silver Platter". Sure,—it is cliche but the "white glove" service and the silver plated pieces can make Formalwear accessories seem even more precious—and tasteful.

Back to the every-day portions—and sizes in the hardware store. The most mundane items take on decorative and desirable attributes when treated with imagination and juxtaposed—off-centered—used in a decidedly different manner. A pile of gleaming nails or screws to contrast with fine leather goods,—a mallet and chisel and some marble chips to suggest a sculpture in progress,—a mannequin loosely bound in coils of copper or brass wire—or coils of wire or gleaming metal scouring pads used to produce impromptu but glistening coiffures. "Take your mitts of"—if they are asbestos kitchen mitts. "Handle With Care"—so handle with color coordinated pot-holders and there are some wonderfully inventive ones out there. "Dip Into—"and dip in with the biggest ladles you can find. In a shadow box,—when you lift that ladle out of the pot—it can be dripping faux pearls—beads—lace-up shoes or boots.

Have you considered all the possibilities in the plastic—see through and not so see through—garment storage bags? The shoe bag that hangs inside the closet door can hang inside a shoe window—filled and overflowing. The accessory bags and plastic boxes—well—that's obvious! Dress your bare,"stripped-for-action" mannequin in a garment bag because everything in the store is on sale. The list is endless, but let's close with the myriad possibilities and unlimited uses the displayperson can have for all those colored, coordinated, and completely accessorized plastic containers and utensils that they might fall heir to—in a Hardware Store.

DETOUR, West Broadway, Soho, New York City
Window Design: Anne Costantini

Rope them in! Lasso the lot—catch them and hold them with rope; cotton rope, hempen rope, flaxen rope, or silken rope. Rapunzel never had it so good or so long as the twisted tresses that drop down into the display set-up left, and gets involved with the two chic, leather and shearling costumes. You can't help but snare the viewer with the composition below. The mannequin has a hold on something and won't let go as she pulls the viewer into the window action. The rope act works "with" rather than "counter" the parts that make up the promotion. Silk and velvet ropes suggest art galleries—fine restaurants—opera and the theater. It's Standing Room Only! White cotton roping is nautical and a natural for sea-going, seasonal designs—with Navy—with red, white and blue—with tars, spars, stars and stripes. So, "Tie one on"—"Pull in a _____"—"Heave to _____"—"Catch a _____" and make a winner.

GUCCI, Fifth Avenue, New York City
Corp. Dir. of Visual Presentation: Guy Scarangello

KAUFMANN'S, Pittsburgh, PA
V.M. Director: David Knouse, V.P.
Downtown Visual Director: Anthony Lucas
Downtown V.M. Manager: Jack Neuser

ANDRE OLIVER, New York City
Visuals Sitarski/Heneks

There is no season on rope, especially for out-of-doors and sports minded fashions. Above: a group of crayon colored sweater outfits are either off to pull someone out of a hole in the ice—or to start a climb up an icy incline. With denim and Western wear—with boots and fringed leather accessories—tooled belts and silver with turquoise jewelry,—coils of rope and wisps of tumbleweed or a cactus plant can provide the desired ambiance—plus elevations and a neutral back-up for merchandise. Rope can involve your mannequins in a maze or a tied-up "Laccoon" composition. Rope can be arranged into a "cats cradle" large enough to swing some mannequins or catch some garments or accessories in a king-sized spider's web made of rope or twine.

Clothes lines are also rope—of a kind—and they can sweep across a display space and show a variety of merchandise "pinned" up with either old fashioned wooden pins or the new colorful plastic ones. Along with clothes lines you'll find laundry baskets and clothes hampers—natural woven reed ones and the brilliant plastic ones (see page 102) that can either sit on the ground or get piled high—or even be sported as head-dresses for washable fashions gone "native". Pots and pans, pails and buckets—silvery galvanized beauties that are there to promote a wash and wear event—to turn into miniature lakes for even more miniature sailboats—or to catch the raindrops in a Rainwear display. Let it rain—let it shine—in either case the pails and buckets will work as props—as elevations—as containers for coordinates. If you prefer a more "modern" way to hang out your washables, there are the wood and rope clothes dryers—in a variety of sizes and styles—that are also great for showing separates and accessories in an assortment window.

KAUFMANN'S, Pittsburgh, PA
V.M. Director: David Knouse, V.P.

B. ALTMAN, Fifth Avenue, New York City
Window Manager: Andrew Druschilowsky
Window Design: David Milutin

GUMP'S, San Francisco, CA
V.M. Director: Robert Mahoney, SVM.

B. ALTMAN, Fifth Avenue, New York City
Window Manager: Andrew Druschilowsky
Window Design: David Milutin

Plug in for special interest! There are loads of lighting fixtures and light lamps to chose from. There are safety lights and drop lights in brilliant orange or attention getting yellow—to bare bulbs hanging down naked—exposed—and getting the shopper's eye. Hang them neatly in a row and let the color of the fixture or the lamp contrast with the merchandise behind or just "Light Up" with color as the accent. Just as exciting are the long, squiggly extension cords that go on yard after yard unraveling and winding in and out—up and around the merchandise and the mannequins. Right: an "electrifying" window where the black cord snakes around on and off the back wall while the background sputters with the excitement of shadows and blobs of colored light. You don't have to see the lamp to know that the "Light is on _____". A row of simple, lamp-shaded bulbs over a row of mannequins adds extra light and emphasis to a neat set-up, while a single, wound up light and cord can, in a shadow box, be all it takes to show small accessories that "Highlight" an outfit.

HIRSHLEIFER'S, Manhasset, NY
Visuals Sitarski/Heneks

BERGDORF GOODMAN, New York City
Director of Design: Angela Patterson, V.P.

MACY'S, Herald Square, New York City
Window Manager: Linda Fargo

ELIZABETH ARDEN, New York City
Display Director: Walter Rummenie

Fluorescents; pencils of light—pointers of illumination—color directionals. The simplest most common of fluorescent fixtures—the ones that were removed and stored away during the last retrofitting can come up out of the basement and take their rightful place in the window; laid on the ground as horizontal bands of cool light or set on an angle for dynamic impact in an otherwise vertical composition. You control the color of the light output by the lamp you chose—from cool, cool white to the yellowish daylight to the deluxe warm whites with the peachy emission. For special color emphasis there are plastic sleeves that slip over the tubes to transform them into glowing rods of yellow—green—red—blue—etc. Don't discard your dead, burnt out lamps. Even they can be used like jack-straws in a display. In addition to the regular 2'-4'- and 6' slender lamps there are the "halos" of fluorescence—the rounders to crown a mannequin or cinch a pillow—outline or frame a clock or some small fashion accessory. Step out in light and remember,—fluorescents are the "inexpensive" source of light but they do pay off with Interest.

BARNEY'S, Chelsea, New York City
Creative Director: Simon Doonan

NIEMAN MARCUS, Beverly Hills, L.A., CA
Window Design: Pala Kersulis

SAVVY ELEVATIONS **ON 4**

HENRI BENDEL, West 57th Street, New York City
Window Design: Danuta Ryder

An "UP" note; Ladders. Try either the kind with rungs between two uprights or the step kind with little risers in an A-frame. Ladders are naturals for "Everything is up"—"Come up to ____"—or "Step up to ____" (with shoes doing the stepping)—"On the rise"—"A new level of ____". The ladders can be left in the neutral wood finish or the aluminum state or sprayed a fashionable accent color—or a deep, dark black. You could even wrap them in tissue and twine or bedeck them with ribbons and streamers. The runged ladders can stretch from the front glass to up the back wall—or stretch horizontally across the window space—or they can be used criss-crossing—a diagonal forest of interlacing ladders. The rectangular openings are small picture frames that can bring out some part of a costume or show up some fashion accessory. The mini-frames also can highlight an assortment of similar but different items like china, glass, silver. The stepped ladders can be used to raise up mannequins—create different levels of interest for groupings or bring merchandise up closer to the shopper's eye level. There are all sorts of architectural possibilities in ladders—just waiting to be tried.

CHARLES JOURDAN, Trump Tower, New York City
Window Design: David Griffin

GIMBELS, New York City
V.M. Director: Bernie Hauserman

SAKS FIFTH AVE., New York City
V.M. Director: Robert Benzio, SVM, V.P.

"Wired for Style". Chicken wire—rabbit wire—expanded mesh—woven or linked—fencing and screening materials—shiny or matte—silvery glints that weave in and out of displays. The lighter weight metal "fabrics" can be unfurled off the roll then swirled—twisted and turned—stretched into an unending variety of configurations that can envelop mannequins or accessories in a silvery haze. The heavier materials are firmer and more rigid and can hold up shoes or even complete outfits up at eye level. The mesh can be sprayed and it is designed to hang things on like Christmas balls—prisms—snowflakes or even irridescent glass spheres that can become the ocean's spray on a crested wire wave in a swimwear window. The mesh can also be laced with colorful shoe laces to complement sneakers racing on semi-invisible inclines—tied with bows —adorned with ribbons or lashed with twine or cotton roping. "Caught in the web of _____", "Enmeshed in _____", or "Caught in the act of _____". The wire mesh trash cans make excellent accompaniments for the panels of mesh that also suggest playgrounds and ball parks.

WILKES BASHFORD, San Francisco, CA
Window Design: Fred Washington

On the following pages: "Cleaning UP"—"Everything must go"—"A Clean Sweep"—"And away they go"—and Sale-Time can be Fun-Time with brooms, mops, dust pans, pails and shovels—and as previously shown—the Vacuum sweepers and cleaners. These props are all designed to set the shopper's mind in the right direction. Kiddie size brooms are the way to go for mini-witches especially if they are boot-bound. A "Welcome Mat" is an invitation to try on some real comfortable—"homey" shoes and also could make a rather unique "placemat" for a high-style or high-

tech arrangement of china and glass. The pushers and pullers of heavy industry can also push and pull their weight as window props. The wheelbarrows are bringing in bits and pieces of the latest in mens' wear while the heavy duty dollys do double duty as props—and also set up an ambiance for casual wear. Scaffolding and oil cans; a setting for denims and "constructed" clothes—the basic elements for elevations and multi-level presentations. It only takes a "hard hat" to accessorize a well-tailored outfit out in the field.

MACY'S, Herald Square, New York City
Window Manager: Linda Fargo

LONIA, West 55th Street, New York City
Window Design: Linda Friedman

LONIA, West 55th Street, New York City
Window Design: Linda Friedman

ANN TAYLOR, East 57th Street, New York City
Window Design: Perrone/Allen

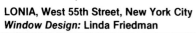

MACY'S, Herald Square, New York City
Window Manager: Linda Fargo

F. BODNER, Town Center, Boca Raton, FL
Window Design: Freddie Bodner

FIORUCCI, East 59th Street, New York City
Window Design: Philip McNaughton

CHARLES JOURDAN, Trump Tower, New York City
Window Design: David Griffin

Garbage cans aren't just for trash. They can add pizzaz to a Back-to-School promotion where the kids are just jumping for joy(?). It is "Urban Style"—it's "City Street Chic"—it's campy class and especially so when the garbage cans are brand new and shiny bright in sprayed enamel, high-gloss colors. Use them as elevations—stack them up—or turn them over and let the good things roll out into sight of the viewer. A graffiti background—and it is a street scene,—a planked white-washed fence and it is suburbia or Backyard Americana. In any case, a stuffed furry cat or two would populate the scene with humor. Forms can be rising out of shiny aluminum cans to show off tops and sweaters while others can be crawling out of overturned cans to show off the bottoms. Don't overlook, as an accessory or as an alternative, all the possibilities inherent in the assorted size trash bags; white, black or olive neutral. They can shroud your mannequins during a Sale when "Everything's Got To Go", or be stylishly draped, shaped and then accessorized when it is the accessories that really count. Think what Halloween can be like with just loads of large white and black trash bags floating off on bent wire hangers!

Also—before we leave mesh completely behind; a quick double take on rigid grids that can be used to trap a mannequin (in an animal print) or show off a great many shoes and handbags. Grids also—like the mesh panels shown framed and unframed on pages 114 and 115 invite the clever displayperson to lace—bind—wind or weave merchandise and accessories through the evenly spaced openings.

FILENE'S, Boston, MA
V.P. Director: Arthur Crispino, V.P.
Boston V.M. Director: Steven Vieser

ROSSETTI, Madison Avenue, New York City
Window Design: Chuck Price

11
Construction

"Rugged"—"Built"—"Constructed"—"Made to Last" are some of the terms associated with building and building materials; with concrete, steel, T-beams and I beams, girders, bricks, and mortar. The same terms refer to classic fashions—elegant styling—outdoor fashions and tailor-made, made-to-order suits. These expressions are suited to suits for the career conscious woman or man—and for the hunting outfits and heavy rugged wear for out-of-doors persons.

To visualize these and many other "constructed" terms one need only visit the local lumber yard and the building materials supplier. In addition to the obvious like planks of wood, 2x2s, 4x4s, lath strips and mold strips, there are the cement blocks, the air or fire blocks, the glass blocks and the bricks of various finishes and colors,—slate for tiling the roof or laying the patio path. The magical dimension of 4x8 conjures up visions of sheets of plywood—fine veneer panels—homosote and plaster boards—and all the other building and finishing panels that can comfortably back up a group of mannequins in a display area.

Getting to the "finishing" end of construction: the endless array of doors and door frames,—from flush to raised panels to carved extravaganzas,—the shutter door—the double dutch door—the louvered door, and all the window frames that go from up and down or side to side—from multi-mullioned to wide expanses yet to be filled with glass. There are the newel posts—the railings—risers and treads of staircases—the wrought iron, wood or sleek stainless spiraling staircases that are contained within a 5' radius and carry mannequins or merchandise up-up-up- to the viewer's eye level. There are also the finely carved moldings—the corbels and the caps,—the pilasters and entablatures that go over doors or roofs.

Outside the house: there are the shutters and the window boxes that by themselves suggest a house—and the window box is waiting to be filled with geraniums and dripping ivy—or maybe shoes and bags sprouting up for Spring.

Before the final painting and papering—the airconditioning, the heating and ventilation systems go in bringing shiny tin, copper and brass pipes, elbows, tees—tinsmith delights and fantasies of metal tubes and cubes and curves. The plumbing suppliers carry many lengths of pipes, including the PVC kind, that, as you will see in this chapter, can be used to make abstract forms to be turned into urban "parks". The plumbing suppliers also carry radiators that we show here, unmasked, as well as the shower heads and faucets that turn gridded masonite 4x8 panels into lavishly tiled pools or shower rooms.

Going out to the back yard: the wooden picket fences of assorted designs—the stockade fences—the heavy cyclone fences—or the rustic caprice of logs with wagon wheels for trim. Some Construction or Building Suppliers even have the easy to set-up "storage bins" that look like miniature "barns" and would be perfect for a kid's playhouse in a children's active sportswear display.

The possibilities are endless; the list of available material goes on and on and they are available to make that "Lasting Impression",—that are "Planned for Success"—or "According to the Plans".

PIZITZ, Birmingham, AL
V.M. Director: **Jim Luker**

JORDAN MARSH, Boston, MA
V.M. Director: Linda Bramlage, V.P.

"Enter into_____"—"Opening Vistas"—"Making an entrance into _____". Doors open the way and lead the viewer inside or outside—wherever the action is. French doors, even unglazed, suggest fine old classic houses where traditional fashions are at home and always welcome to come in and be seen. Left: a pattern of doors—no walls—just doors and one afloat. It becomes a decorative setting for white nautical separates trimmed in navy, emerald and yellow. Above: a mood of mystery and suspense of "Who dunnit?" in Jordan Marsh's window; eerie blue, low lighting, and framed doors with fan windows on top. The muslin drapes shroud the white wicker furniture and even one of the mannequins. Another kind of door—a paneled one—opens into the city street just right for the citified, tailored suit. The wire outline sculpture is an extra nicety but it is the door that backs up the mannequin and sets the scene. On page 120, Construction is going on because the bride is "Building for the Future"—and the contrast of crepe against concrete—and lace against lath gets attention.

LORD & TAYLOR, New York City
New York Visual Merchandise Director: **Ken Schleimann**

GIMBELS, New York City
V.M. Director: Bernie Hauserman

Lath strips or trellises—ready made or made-to-order; simple shoji-like panels without rice paper fillers can become multi-mullioned windows that suggest a country home with a garden view—or the panels can just float in a white space as an abstract design for costumers to loom through, hangers to hang from and accessories to set on and loop through. Trellises are also available with lozenge shaped openings and become espalier supports—stand up under the weight of climbing vines and flowering wisterias, —or the panels can back up garden sculpture or be arranged into skeletal gazebos. These lightweight constructions—usually available in modules like 2'x8', 4'x8' and 4'x4' are just as effective as semi-dividers in open back windows as they are on the selling floor—on platforms and ledges. A panel plus a single chair, a length of fabric and maybe a potted plant—instant "room".

HIGBEES, Cleveland, OH
V.M. Director: Frank Valore, V.P.

JORDAN MARSH, Boston, MA
V.M. Director: Linda Bramlage, V.P.
Boston Visuals Director: Carl Russo

LORD & TAYLOR, New York City
New York Visual Merchandise Director: Ken Schleimann

A vignette setting simply sketches out a place—a time or a look. It leaves much for the viewer to fill in from her own background—her own dreams or memories. Here are two subtley, well done vignettes that use the picket fence to set the stage. Above: on an "icy" floor these little girls in velvet, lace and bunny fur are skating. Bare branches suggest the wintertime and the white washed pickets recall a bye-gone era—a wistful look back to another century when designs like these were worn by rich little girls. Right: resting on an Adirondack chair is a stylish lady of today in a crisp red and white outfit. The chair, the fence, and the post behind are mottled in pink on white—gracefully aged and antiqued to suggest the worn refinement of the Hamptons. The plants fill in as colorful details but the setting is still vague enough for any shopper to change the venue and see it her way.

SAKS FIFTH AVE., New York City
V.M. Director: Robert Benzio, SVM, V.P.

SONIA RYKIEL, Madison Ave., New York City
Window Designer: Marc Manigualt

VITTORIO RICCI, Columbus Avenue, New York City
Window Design: Marc Manigault

Architectural elements and building blocks will tell a story that can be Urban—or that can make a "Lasting Impression". It is like the contrast of materials that opened this chapter—the unexpected twosomes—rough textures with finely finished products that appear more finished and fine for the contrast. It is the divine contrasted with the profane—the sublime with the down-to-earth. Cinder blocks—concrete blocks—bricks—fire blocks—sand and lime—I-beams and T-beams—textured steel floor plates—they all proclaim the tough, rugged ways of labor and construction; a contrast to elegant imported leathers, soft suedes and cashmere coats. The cinder blocks, shown here, serve as an elevation for the mannequin, above, and below; a series of build-ups for the shoes. On the right: a more sophisticated "building block"—glass blocks that also recall the 30s and the 40s—Moderne and Modernistic—and that today is once again becoming a surfacing material of choice for shops, stores and class restaurants. In this composition they "tumble" through space—adding a touch of sparkle to a presentation of black suits and dresses. In shadow boxes and cases, these attractive, hollow glass cubes could work with cosmetics—costume jewelry—and of course, shoes, bags and belts or built up semi-partitions. You could try opening one or two—and sealing a small bauble inside.

ANN TAYLOR, E. 57th Street, New York City
Window Design: Perrone/Allen

SONIA RYKIEL, Madison Avenue, New York City
Window Designer: **Marc Manigualt**

ELIZABETH ARDEN, New York City
Display Director: **Walter Rummenie**

From the Plumbing Suppliers we bring in the sink—the bathroom sink to create an intimate—very intimate and off-beat setting for lingerie and the underneath story. Imagine what you could do with the proverbial "kitchen sink" to show off fine china, glasswear and silver? It is the unexpected that stops the shopper in the street—so why not everything including the kitchen sink (see page 64). What about the pipes; those long, vertical lengths of cast iron—of copper—of brass—of steel,—the flanges that go with the pipes—the connections—the "T"'s, the "L"'s the whole alphabet of twists and angles that can turn the vertical pipes into strange, out-of-this-world forests—or into sophisticated T-shaped drapers. The Sonia Rykiel window, left, snares a wayward branch, still enriched with a few, fast-fading leaves, within the black clamp that encircles the pipe—and the setting is a sleek, steely city-like "forest" of naked trees. On the right: The Liz Claiborne separates are attractively presented on the pipes that are finished in white and flanged into the floor of the window. Here, it is the PVC tubing that provides the crisp, white finish.

Pipes and clamps can become the recognizable background seamless paper holders one associates with photographer's studios (see page 190). They are "construction" materials which can be used to make abstract settings that not only show mannequins at various levels (page 117)—they can hold merchandise within their silvery vertical, horizontal and diagonal lines.

KAUFMANN'S, Pittsburgh, PA
V.M. Director: David Knouse, V.P.
Downtown Visual Director: Anthony Lucas

Shower heads—faucets—spigots—nozzles—things that "Turn On"—that you can "Shower with ____" or "Tape in ____" also come from the Plumbing Supplies Area. Right: grid incised masonite panels look enough like white ceramic tiles to become a pool enclosure and the shower head and faucet provide the "details". The Shower Room and the adjacent Locker Room are great places to show off men and women in their undergarments—in their active sportswear—or to promote body-covering towels during a white sale. They are the natural habitat for work-out clothes. Kids could romp and stomp under a shower head "flowing" forth a cellophane stream—while they show off their new swim suits.

GIMBELS, New York City
V.M. Director: Bernie Hauserman

129

LA MARCA, East 57th Street, New York City
Window Design: Marc Manigault

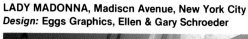

LADY MADONNA, Madiscn Avenue, New York City
Design: Eggs Graphics, Ellen & Gary Schroeder

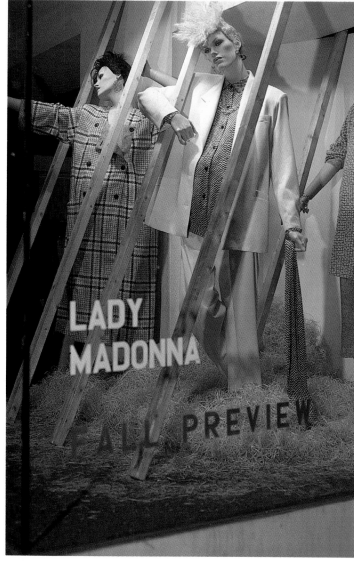

From the Lumberyard: nice, clean planks of wood—lengths of 1x2—1x3—2x4—knotty and not so knotty—pine, birch, oak. Unadorned and unvarnished they can become saw-horses or even make believe horses to support an array of Western accessories, or with some planking on top and maybe some blue-prints to cover the surface—we are on a construction site—and the well dressed man in the "constructed" suit is an architect or an engineer. Right: a bairn-to-be in a barn raising setting. It's all illusion, but the leaning lengths of lumber do suggest a structure going up. The neutral beige tones of the wood blend with the colors of the clothes—and the sawdust and straw strewn floor.

4x4 posts are nailed together to form 8' letters that spell out K*E*N*Z*O—across the Madison Avenue windows. The letters are both a background and a constant reminder of whose designs are being presented on the articulated, wood cut-out forms. It's so simple—it has to work! The natural wood planks lean against the two vertical strips that span the window. One plank has been moved aside so that the mannequin can sit in the open space. The leaning board directs the viewer down to the neatly arranged red and yellow merchandise on the neutral floor. Barely visible—some greenery sneaks through the break in the fence.

BON GENIE, Lausanne, Switzerland

KENZO, Madison Avenue, New York City

ELIZABETH ARDEN, New York City
Display Director: Walter Rummenie

"Heat Up" the scene with a radiator. Whether it is to promote new, warm winter suits and furs—or to play up a cheery, cherry red Christmas gift of nightgowns for him and for her,—a lowly radiator will do it. So, take it out from its mesh enclosure—reveal it in shiny black or radiant red. In both settings, the heating device is the only prop in the setting and yet it does steam up the mood and get the message across. Below: metal pipe saw-horses instead of the familiar wooden ones hold up the black table top that serves as an elevation in this extra tall window. The bright red enamel ties in with the hearty emphasis on red in the fashions on view.

CHARLES JOURDAN, Trump Tower, New York City
Window Design: Robert and Steven Balavender

MADIGANS, Yorktown, IL
Visuals Director: J.D. Marshall
Visual Manager: Darre F. Loyd

CASTNER KNOTT, Nashville, TN
V.M. Director: Elaine Helnsley

LIFE'S LITTLE PRIVILEGES, Great Neck, NY

H.V.A.C. = D. Heating, Ventilation, Air Conditioning, plus Imagination will equal DISPLAY! From the tinsmith's shop—from the friendly air-conditioner installers come the round tubes—the elbows—the vents—the rectangular lengths—and they all work to promote outfits for when its warm or when its cold. You can make your twisted and turned creations that shimmer and shine in your windows—or you can even construct a "tin man" to delight smaller viewers. Just add a Dorothy-ishly dressed mannequin—a big stuffed plush lion with a crown—a Toto-ish furry pup and "We're off ____".

More examples of PVC pipes and tubes are presented; one for rugged shoes—the other for children's wear—and they both work effectively.

GIMBELS, New York City
V.M. Director: Bernie Hauserman

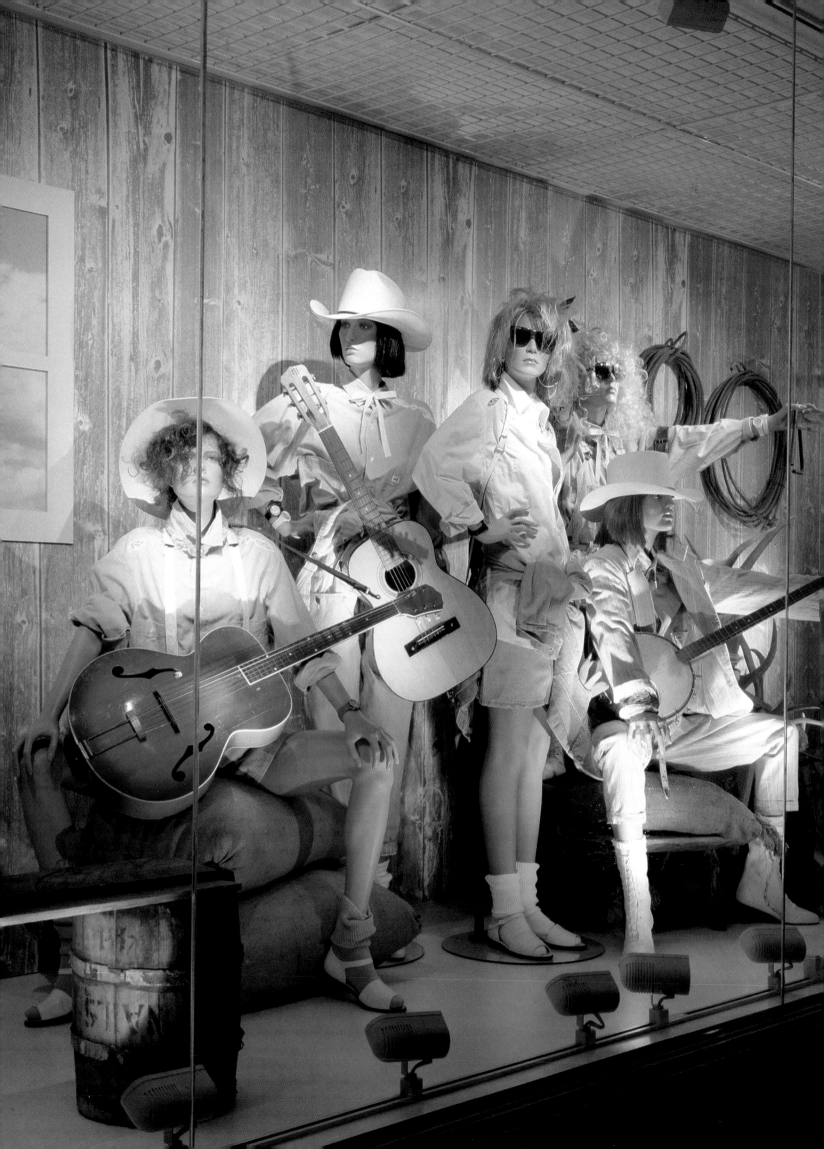

12
Music

A musical flourish to herald a new season: an arpeggio—a trumpet's blare—the rat-a-tat-tat of the snare drum—the boom-boom-boom of the bass drum,—a chord that strikes a chord and ties together a product with an image. The Music Store is more than a source for trumpets, tubas, horns and bassoons—of violins, violas and cellos—and the occasional big, bass violin,—of flutes and piccolos, and grand pianos. It is also the place to get: music stands—simple, collapsible wire ones or ornate brass stands or elegant wood turned ones. There are musical manuscripts of love-songs—patriotic songs—foreign songs—and holiday songs, as well as the simple lined sheets just waiting to carry musically inspired copy lines. Some stores also carry records as well as recorders and record players. You may even find the materials there to turn your window into a recording studio with mikes, sound equipment, synthesizers, electric guitars—and a few folding chairs to complete the Session in progress.

The Record Stores sometimes have "dummy" covers of top or hot recording stars that you can borrow,—or you can contact the Record Companies and get their "point of purchase" and promotional kits to use in your windows or on the ledges.

If you have the budget—and the time—you might scout the second hand shops—the Salvation Army stores—the Pawn Shops for instruments past their playing prime that you can own and have on call for the many different times and different ways you can use them. You might also approach the school bands—the marching societies—the music schools for their discards or about-to-become discards. They may no longer make sweet music or play in tune, but nobody will know that when they see them in a set-up, mute but effective.

Musical instruments, of course, go with formalwear but they also go with uniforms and the same sources that supply band instruments may have some brass buttoned beauties to lend out for a window airing for Sale events—Anniversaries—Fourth of July—President's Day, etc. You don't need all of the 76 trombones to set hearts and spirits soaring—one player per window redolent in crimson, gold and white will do it—or any other patriotic color scheme will do it. Uniforms go with flags and banners and whether they are the Stars and Stripes—or State or City flags—School Flags—or the flags of friendly nations—they do get the excitement—and color—going. All it takes is an out-of-view breeze to stir the silk—make it flap and flutter—and what a way to march into a red/white/and blue promotion—a navy event—or even an institutional set-up. There are flag and banner makers listed in the Yellow Pages with a wealth of multi-hued silks waiting to be unfurled to the accompaniment of an un-tapped drum or the non-blasted trumpet. In a window, Silence is golden when the silence is from gleaming, golden instruments.

M.G.A., Beverly Hills, CA
Window Designer: **Chris Jonic**

BLOOMINGDALE'S, New York City
V.M. Director: Colin Birch

LORD & TAYLOR, New York City
New York Visual Merchandise Director: Ken Schleimann

"They're playing our song". There is music in the air—and the melody lingers on season after season after season. A string trio to start off this musical collection; violins and violas from the music store along with some lovely brass and wrought iron music stands to complete the setting. Little girls' frilly, lacy, white and pink dresses make their debut with violas at hand. It is a recital and you know they will do well in their dress-to-succeed outfits. Music goes with romance and the blushing pink romantic dresses on the two mannequins above sings in the pink glow of light. The candle holders on the antique stands light up the love theme. Instead of music sheets on the stands there could have been especially selected accessories; scarves—small bags—silk flowers. Without the mannequins, the stands alone could star in an all accessory quartet. Right: A Little Night Music—not by Mozart but by La Lingerie in silky satins and lace. Here too the violins provide the mannequins with an action that also happen to prop-out the setting.

LA LINGERIE, Madison Avenue, New York City
Window Design: Diane Tucker

136

La Lingerie

MAXFIELD'S, Melrose Avenue, Los Angeles, CA
Window Design: **Simon Doonan**

Moving over to the Brass and Wind sections for a change of pace and tempo. Jazzy, blues notes take over and we're swinging low and mellow. The saxophones in Maxfield's display add a subtle shimmer to a cool blue/black presentation. The "shades" on the mannequins and the berets are reminiscent of Paris Blues of the 60s. Tiffany toot-toots its tribute to the diamond necklace being offered by the silver instrument and the music sheet carries the orchestration for the salute. The two displays on the right seem to not only be indebted to the local H.S. marching bands—but the concept does honor to a clever Busby Berkley musical production number that was created for Ann Miller—back in the 50s. Barneys window has the whole orchestra playing back up for the sultry chanteuse in sequined black. This was a holiday window and there is no doubt that there is something to celebrate. The Christmas ornaments in the background are the only give-away. Below: She's "Stepping Out" alright,—in tune with the clarinets. Here, too, only 'bits' of the players are shown; it is the instruments that carry the melody and make the magic and the music fuse. The top hats and red bowties are a clever designer's touch that reinforces the "dress-up" and "go out" theme of the window. The blue filtered light is also evident in these displays.

TIFFANY'S, Fifth Avenue, New York City
Window Design: **Gene Moore**

138

BARNEY'S, Chelsea, New York City
V.M. Director: Guy Scarangello
Window Manager: Nando Miglio

JORDAN MARSH, Boston, MA
V.M. Director: Robert Unger, V.P.

FERRAGAMO, Fifth Avenue, New York City

GLORIA PRET A PORTER, Montreal, Quebec, Canada
Decors: Yves Guilbeault

An elegant setting for menswear—or any fine merchandise— for Christmas; the Ferragamo window, left, strikes the right note. The fine, old mandolin rests against the Biedermeier chair in the midst of an eclectic melange of antiques and near antiques that are unified by the warm color of the wood that glows in the soft light. Tossed about—like the sheets of manuscript—are the fashionable gift suggestions. A single, bee-lit tree in a terra-cotta planter provides the seasonal note.

For fashion of a martial stripe, one marches in time to the band. A giant pseudo keyboard fills the gray flannel covered floor and the mannequins, in black and silver, get a real send off against the collage of music sheets that tumble down from the beribboned trumpet that tops the display.

Black notes on white lined sheets can be all the background you need for small cases and shadow boxes when you're promoting black and white accessories. Musical instruments—even miniature or children's toys plus music sheets can be the right note to strike for perfumes, cosmetics and jewelry.

MARSHALL FIELD, Chicago, IL
V.M. Director: Homer Sharp, SVM

"Show Time"; time to get into the spotlight and strut your stuff. You're all dressed for the occasion. This corner window becomes the stage,—the grand piano fills the center space and also provides a "Helen Morgan" perch for the lady in red. The two in black and white share the microphone and the long electric cable wends its way through the window. The star spattered background—the theatrical lighting says—"You're on"—so go into your act.

It's Music! You don't strum it—blow it—or tweak it—you have to feed it to get the music. The glitter-glow—the shimmer and shine of the old Juke boxes produce pure nostalgia in windows and in interiors. Left: strings of 45 records hang down and border the window glass but its the illuminated Juke Box that gets all the requests —and fills the demand. Below: It is like walking into a 50s Sweet Shoppe in middle America—something out of American Graffiti. The setting is the selling floor at The Limited and the shopper is invited to wander in and become part of the tableau. In addition to the musical programmer, there are the wire framed ice-cream chairs and tables that everyone remembers—or thinks they do,—plus merchandise to pick up and peruse. No doubt about it—"A stroll down memory lane"—and they are playing our song.

CASTNER KNOTT, Nashville, TN
V.M. Director: **Elaine Hensley**

THE LIMITED, Madison Avenue, New York City
V.M. Director: **Chris Dixon**

JACKSON

GEMINI MANNEQUINS

133W25 STREET NEW YORK NY 10001   TEL: 212 242 0374/5988   TELEX: 4971553 GEMINI
23/25 KENSINGTON PARK ROAD LONDON W11   TEL: 01-229 3843   TELEX: 24773 GEMS G

13
Photography

"Get in the Fashion Picture"—"Snap It"—"Click". Photography equipment is so much a part of the Fashion scene—and the reportage of what is new—who is doing what—and where it is happening. Cameras record the special moments. They suggest the ephemeral quality of fashion—that must be caught at once or the moment is gone. Cameras can be the big, boxy affairs on tripods complete with black drop cloth that can either be so antique as to "Tintype" an heirloom style Wedding gown and that "Special Moment"—or so state-of-the-art to be used by a long haired, avant-garde photographer of today. In between there are the Brownies—the sporty colorful plastic cases that float, swim and all but take their own pictures—the instamatics—and the Polaroids with their at-once prints. "Look What's Developing". "The Living Proofs"—"Negative and Positive"—"Capture the Moment"— "Hold the Memory" of "A Day to Remember".

Along with the hosts of cameras are the lights that one associates with the Art of Photography, and the unending, restless black coils of electric wires. "Plug-In"—"Light Up the Scene". "High Lights and Shadows"—"In the Spotlight". To control that light one has all those reflectors and deflectors— the silvery umbrellas and the white umbrellas—the barndoor flaps on the spotlight housings. Tripods can be used as elevations to hold fashion accessories off the ground—with or without the cameras. Film cannisters can be split open to reveal even more fashion accessories; "We Have It in Black And White" or "In Glorious Color". For shadow box windows and cases; the rolls of film—or contact sheets—or strips of developed negatives can swirl and eddy in with the baubles, the bags, belts and shoes.

For an interesting effect—bring some light boxes into the window to either back light up some large photo transparencies or special prints, or just to leave empty but use them to back up black dresses or suits for a striking silhouette presentation. The same light boxes that the photographer uses to check out his films, slides and negatives can be converted into platforms to show fine china, glass and crystal with the light coming up through the frosted sheet to make the merchandise sparkle. "Check Out These Details". "Picture Perfect"—"Needs No Retouching".

The whole TV industry can be invited to come into your windows to "Spread the Newest". Borrow some of their outdated "back-up" cameras and equipment to fill your display space with the excitement of "Saturday Night Live".

Rolls of seamless paper hung on black pipe frames suggest a photographer's studio and the various hues, shades and tints of the wide, wide paper offer endless possibilities for contrast or for coordination with color promotions. A chrome yellow promotion—especially with black accessories—would be a natural for a tie-in with Kodak and all its products and world recognized packaging.

In this chapter we only lightly touch on a very popular cliche but one that can be expanded upon as a Fashion expression; the Motion Pictures—the movies—Hollywood. It is the movie camera—kleig lights—the clap-board banded in black and white that snaps before each scene and is recorded on in chalk—the director with his name-stenciled-on, canvas chair—the old time megaphone—the sound recording equipment. So much of this material can be rented or borrowed—or just "faked" in your own shop.

So "Lights, Actions, Camera"—and every mannequin becomes a model and every model a salesperson wrapped in glamour and beauty.

B. ALTMAN, Fifth Avenue, New York City
Window Manager: **Andrew Druschilowsky**
Window Design: **David Milutin**

FILENE'S, Boston, MA
V.P. Visual Merchandising: Arthur Crispino

Lights! Action! CAMERA! Photos and Photographers—light bulbs and adjustable light stands—silver and white umbrellas to reflect or deflect the light—the excitement of the Fashion shoot—a filmed commercial—the end result of roll after roll being shot and developed. A tribute to the photographer—the chronicler of What's New. On page 144—You are there. A designer's new line is being photographed for a fashion magazine layout. You know it because you can see the photographer setting up the equipment, and the rack of clothes who are to be the stars of the issue. Below: it is what you don't see that makes it so tantalizing. Behind the brilliant blast of "The New Creators" are mannequins in the hottest, new clothes being photographed. The white floor and walls and the attendant equipment tells you so. Left and Right: the results of the shoot become the background and foreground for Black & White—or "Positive & Negative" promotions—as well as of-the-moment accessories. You know something is developing on the right from the clipped on—unretouched prints that are casually but carefully arranged into a composition with belts and shoes mixed in.

MACY'S, Herald Square, New York City
Window Manager: Linda Fargo

MACY'S, Herald Square, New York City
Window Manager: Linda Fargo

JORDAN MARSH, Boston, MA
V.M Director: Robert Unger, V.P.

BERGDORF GOODMAN, New York City
Director of Design: Angela Patterson, V.P.

Photography equipment plus photographs suggest the stir and stimulation of Hollywood—the theatre—glamour—the ultimate in chic. The neatly arranged row of "stars" balances the scurry and sweep of the black power lines coiling around the "Opening Night" message on the floor. Row after row after row of contact sheets—in black and white—become the sophisticated patterned back-up for the glamourous black outfit with the subtlest of sheens. It's not important what the miniature photos are of—what is important is that they imply—and how well they lend themselves to supporting the star performer.

Even persons who have never witnessed a shoot recognize the white cotton umbrella—or the silvery ones—and know what they are used for—even if they don't know how they work. So, when a clever displayperson turns a square scarf into a light reflector,—the shopper out in the street recognizes the clamp-on pole and the lights and naturally assumes what the scarf represents. The expert lighting and the sun-glasses help.

148

JORDAN MARSH, Boston, MA
V.M. Director: Linda Bramlage, V.P.

HENRI BENDEL, West 57th Street, New York City
Window Design: Danuta Ryder

149

Photographs and film strips; the opaque and the transparent—color and black and white. The famous, familiar model's face becomes the only face to show off this line of separates. The photograph is superimposed over the mannequin's face and the wig is artfully arranged to finish off the face framing tresses that are part of the picture. Below: a heroic sized roll of film strip becomes the setting and the background for this on-the-selling-floor display. The make-believe, old movie camera out of a Keystone Cops comedy is the prop that turns one kid into a director while the rest "act out" the fashion scenario. Other familiar cliches to further the illusion: the metal film cannisters and the clap-board—and whoever has seen a movie-within-a-movie knows what they represent. In shadow boxes and cases, rolls and rolls of actual film strips could create a black/white spaghetti excitement for small fashion accessories—perfumes—colognes—things that go with "Make-up"—"In the picture"—"Take One"—or any recent movie title can be adapted as a copy line; "Fatal Attraction".

MACY'S, Herald Square, New York City
Window Manager: Linda Fargo

THE BROADWAY, Pasadena, CA
V.M. Director: Doug Leaman, V.P.

SYLVOR CO., INC.

DECORATIVE DISPLAYS SINCE 1929

G-507

WE HAVE THE CAPABILITY TO CREATE, DEVELOP
AND PRODUCE IDEAS TO YOUR SPECIFICATIONS.
WOODWORK - SILK SCREEN - ART - DESIGN

126-11th Avenue NYC, N.Y. 10011 at 20th St. (212) 929-2728

14
Sporting Goods

You don't have to think Sporting Goods Supplies and Gym equipment just for active sportswear and special sporting clothes. There are many other fashion-aware clothes that can benefit from the scale—the shape—and the copy tie-ins that abound in the Sporting Goods area. Finely tailored clothes can get in an extra jab with "In Shape"—"Champion Construction"—"Fit Condition"—or "Prime Condition". The incongruity of two well-dressed, business suited mannequins "weighing-in" on a stand upscale—with boxing gloves on is sure to get a double take from the viewer out in the street. In this chapter we show different ways to punch out a knockout display with material from the boxing arena.

There are row boats and canoes for lacy white cotton dress-ups for summer. All it needs is a few willow branches dripping from above—or spanish moss framing the window. Sail boats would work for pull-ons and pullovers, for active sportswear and swim suits. The colorful sails that add so much pizzazz to the lake scene can be used as drapes—as swags—pulled back prosceniums—curtains or backdrop cloths. You can really take off with the technicolor spectacles—the Windsurfers—that are just right for windows or ledges. They provide the total setting; the attraction—the scale and the color. The mannequins fit right onto them—and off they go. Get an electric fan, moving behind the proscenium—and watch the graphic sails billow in the easy blow.

On a smaller scale, but still colorful and aquatic are the rafts and floats—and all the inflatable accessories from beach balls to pool lounges down to a gaggle of rubber duckies. And just think of what all these take-to-water props could do for a Rainwear promotion.

Coming up on land—unless you've got your hip boots on; "Catch the Big One"—"The Record Catch"—"Don't Let These Get Away". To make sure you land the big one—try the fishing and angling supplies; the rods and reels—the kreels—the nets and flies.

For a real class act: "En Garde". Masks and fencing epees are tres chic—especially if the duelists are bedecked in their best furs. For Valentine's Day—get "Right To The Heart" with fencing gear—the mask, the epee and the padded chest guard with the red heart on it. Your dueling partners could be dressed in crisply tailored suits—"Rapier Sharp" or "On The Cutting Edge".

The All-American sport of Baseball is a springtime phenomenon—like forsythia and the red, red robin. A few balls and bats—a catcher's mitt and mask and "Strike One"—"Safe"—"A Home Run" —"Touches All Bases"—"Batting a Thousand"—"Rooting for the Home Team" (An American Made promotion)—or "Take Me Out To The Ballgame" for spring into summer dress-ups. The scoreboard can really give your fashion team a slew of runs batted in—especially if your coordinates are "Team-mated". Baseball can give you a "Perfect Score". And,—while on teams—let's really Root for the home team; the local colleges and high schools. Get them to lend you their trophies—show off their colors—or, if possible, tie in the local heroes colors with your color promotions—"Really Winners". The school's cheerleaders' pom-poms will add real spirit to Fall and Back to School promotions; add the pennants and banners. Let us not forget the Little League teams and the Soccer teams. They can lead to big league displays—and publicity for the store. Don't take "sides"—but play the odds to win—and show them all.

As you peruse the next several pages you will find some other sporting goods that have much to recommend them for display use.

JORDAN MARSH, Boston, MA
V.M. Director: **Robert Unger, V.P.**

NORTH BEACH LEATHER, Madison Avenue, New York City
Window Design: David Bradescu

Moving in—zooming in—Revving up for action. Motorbikes and scooters are usually black, sleek and shiny vehicles that suggest a life-style—a dashing, daring, devil may care attitude that shows even in the clothes one wears. Whether its flag waving colors—or the zip-zap, snappy style of the clothes—the way out or way in way to go, the easily borrowed or rented motorbike/scooter can fly through a window or interior display and leave the viewers gasping at what just went by. North Beach Leather is taking off in red leather and has a male mannequin straddling the bike and his passenger is riding side-saddle. The other mannequin is cheering them on. Bloomingdales uses the flambouyant red bike as a draper or costumer—to show off a coordinated outfit with accessories to spare.

On page 152, in the Jordan Marsh window, a semi-realistic mannequin heads down the yellow striped road—right towards the shopper out in the street—on a white-washed bike. It is almost like a George Seigal sculpture—white on white except for the blue jacket and the small life-saver that key in with the red, white, and blue merchandise in the display. Note the cut-out in the white back wall that allows the displayperson to use the effective, face-on approach in this shallow window area. The same yellow road lines run up the pedestals that carry the suit forms.

BLOOMINGDALE'S, New York City
V.P. Visual Merchandising: Colin Birch

154

WOODARD & LOTHROP, Washington, DC
Div. V.P. Visual Merchandising: Jack Dorner
Washington V.M. Director: Jan Suit

SAKS FIFTH AVE., New York City
V.M. Director: Robert Benzio, SVM, V.P.

Put on the gloves—take off your robe and come out slugging. A group of knock-out ideas that come from the training camps of champions and contenders. The props are so simple to get—so easy to recognize and they lend themselves to active sportswear—to lingerie and even a fur sale. A couple of white cotton ropes strung across the window glass and we have placed the mannequins in the ring. Towels, pails, a stool or two—satin robes and sneakers complete the image. If you are still developing the Punch-line—you can show the punching bag and put the gloves on the mannequins who are in fighting form—and the outfits are sure to pack a whallop. If the theme is wild and wacky tropical fruit and flower prints—the Fruit-Punch is a clever, punny, funny concept to develop and all it takes to "deliver" the message is a pair of padded gloves on the tough and ready mannequin. The adjectives scattered about in the above copy could easily be used to describe menswear along with—"In Prime Condition"—"Raring to Go."—"The New One-Two"—"The Winner and Still Champion".

LEVEL 1, Condida, Puerto Rico
Window Design: Frank Caballero

FRED THE FURRIER, Fifth Avenue, New York City
Window Design: Michael Landry

On the following pages we take to the snow and the slopes for winter sportswear—outerwear—and furs. All it takes to transport the mannequins and the viewers to Aspen—St. Moritz or any local ski-slide is a floor covered with crushed styro snow—some snowflakes on the glass—on the back wall and anywhere in between, and courtesy of your own sports department or the ski-shop down the road—some skis and poles. The mannequins can stand—walk—sit or collapse and, as in the fur sale window, just get buried in the "snow" with just legs and skis visible to bring home the point. In a shadow box, a spiked ski pole thrust into a snow mound could be all the setting one would want for mittens, scarves and hats to keep off wintry winds. It's "Easy Going"—"On the Fast Track"—"When the Snow Blows"—; that's when the skis and poles come out and slaloming starts in display spaces.

GARFINKELS, Washington, DC
V.M. Director; R.J. Lester

MADIGANS, Yorktown, IL
Visuals Director: J.D. Marshall
Window Manager: Darre F. Loyd

N JANUARY, MY FUR PRICES GO DOWNHILL

FRED THE FURRIER, Fifth Avenue, New York City
Window Design: Michael Landry

FILENE'S, Boston, MA
V.M. Director: Arthur Crispino, V.P.

Fast take-offs for Sporty put-ons! Whether it's a skate board that moves acrobatic kids into school upside down, —or surf boards that sweep into shore in Summer outfits,— the sports supply shop is loaded with the props that will take you—and your shoppers there. The skateboards don't have to be flying in midair—nor do the mannequins need to be quite so active to get the viewers attention. An otherwise empty skateboard could roll into view with a lay down of coordinates or accessories—or imagine a sneaker window with sneakers lined with colorful sports-sox—flying through the window on suspended skateboards,—no legs—no mannequins—just sneakers.

And, what goes with skateboards like the Walkman ear sets and the boom-boxes jiving with music that is all part of the scene. The boom-box could also move out to the beach scene (lower left) where sand and surf blend against a background graphic of beach balls and umbrellas. In addition to surf boards there is all that underwater equipment to use with swim suits and beachwear; the snorkling gear—the inflated vests—the goggles and flippers. Sand on the floor—blue lights on the background and the window is set except for sporting equipment to prop out the display. Where the expert displayperson makes his or her special contribution is in the shaping and draping of the clothes on the mannequins and forms that shows the body in action—and the wind blowing.

KAUFMANN'S, Pittsburgh, PA
V.M. Director: David Knouse, V.P.
Downtown Visual Director: Anthony Lucas

M.G.A., Beverly Hills, CA
Window Designer: Chris Jonic

GIMBELS, New York City
V.M. Director: Bernie Hauserman

JORDAN MARSH, Boston, MA
V.M. Director: Robert Unger, V.P.

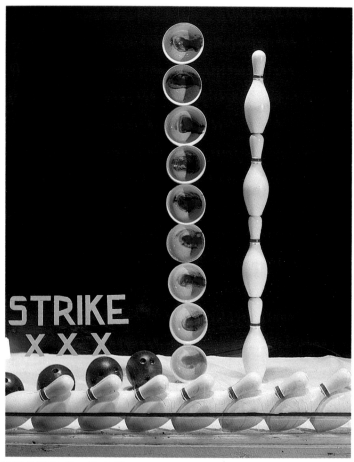

MAD MONK, New York City
Window Design: George N. Shimko

"On Target"—"Take Aim on ____"—"Bulls Eye"—. A great gimmick to score points with is archery equipment—with or without the target. Arrows—with or without the bow—point out special features—suggest speed—direction—movement. They are super directionals! Not only can they do a William Tell bit with apples pierced with arrows, they get to the heart of the matter for Valentine's day and add an excitement of diagonals to a small case or shadow box—with a direct strike on the fashion accessories being featured. Talking of strikes,—what about bowling balls and bowling pins to "bowl them over"—literally as in this ceramic bowl display, but why not in any fashion accessory window? Small pieces of jewelry like bracelets, chains and bangles could be draped on the pins while the bowling balls could add volume and contrast for a perfect score with perfumes and cosmetics. In red and white—you could even bowl her over for Valentine's day. They can also rack up high score for small Father's Day gifts—or menswear, in general.

EDDIE BAUER, San Francisco, CA

Camping Out! A whole way of life that takes with it a whole wardrobe of outer and under wear. Pitch a tent and you have a background and a setting. A grass mat could enhance the scene along with a few birch branches. Along with the tent there are the collapsible chairs—quickie cooking stoves or a rock pile if you prefer to make your own—the sleeping bags—the back pack (maybe open and showing off more merchandise)—the instant shower or maybe—from your local taxidermist—a friendly bear who

has come to visit. Camping equipment could also provide the setting for safari clothes—for the ever-growing, popular beige and khaki "Banana Republic" type cottons and crushed linens. It lends itself to menswear—to womenswear—to children's wear—it can be a Family Affair. The tent and sleeping bags could be a novel way of showing children's sleepwear; a night of "camping out" on the front lawn—or on the living room rug.

B. ALTMAN, Fifth Avenue, New York City
Window Manager: **Andrew Druschilowsky**

A real catch! or—A reel Catch! With a net basket it can be butterflies or fresh fish. Below: in a shallow window a collection of nets—shrimp, fish and butterfly—along with rustic chairs—cars—reels and rods—picnic baskets and even an old trunk. On the back wall: a framed group of prized catches—the ones that didn't get away. The diagonals in the composition—the fishing rods and the oars provide action and vitality for the two abstract figures in blue. Above: in a small window, the net baskets are scooping up swim trunks that are floating by—but they could as easily be bringing in a catch of cosmetics—sports shoes—small bags—jewelry. A single net in a small window where some sand has been scattered on the ground could also do.

Let's get on to dry land for the butterflies and the light, color and loveliness that butterflies are all about. Catch a scarf in a net with a butterfly resting on the rim. Drop some butterflies into your window and arm your mannequins with nets to "Catch the color of ____" these fragile fly-bys. Make it a "Prized Collection"—a "One of a Kind" find—a "Don't let this one get away" display— with nets to get the message across.

LAURA ASHLEY, East 57th Street, New York City
V.M. Director: **Barbara Kleber**

STORES OF THE YEAR
BOOK 4

A Pictorial Report on Store Interiors

STORES OF THE YEAR/Book 4 is a Book of Discoveries. It is about stores—large and small—and very small—that are unique, special, different and exciting. These stores feature designs that stimulate the shopper—and sales. Some are basically "traditional" but with a new quality—a new use of familiar materials or unfamiliar materials shaped to classic forms. Other shops are bright, sparkling, innovations —full of fresh vitality and a joie de vivre.

In this Book of Discoveries—over **250 photos from over 60 stores are reproduced in full color**—you will find experimental design concepts side by side with adaptations of 18th Century motifs—Art Deco derivatives and post Post-Modernism. The fixturing, like the decor, goes from "safe" to audacious, and the newest lighting techniques are presented for the viewer's perusal. Wherever and whenever possible, we have included schematic floor plans of the shops, as well as **comprehensive lists of the store designers, architects, consultants and suppliers.**

Selection of the photographs and editorial commentary were made by Martin M. Pegler, a recognized authority in design and visual presentation.

STORES OF THE YEAR/BOOK 4 is a large format **9"x12" hard-bound picture book with 192 pages and over 250 color photos.** Previous volumes in this collection have become a standard reference for the retail industry, therefore, **no retailer, developer, architect or designer can afford to be without this book.**

The color reproduction will enable you to grasp a feeling of "being there"—even when you're not!

$44.95
ISBN 0-934590-22-2

Here are the stores featured:

BARNEY'S, New York, NY
MISS JACKSON, Tulsa, OK
THE LIMITED, New York, NY
HUMPS, Bal Harbour, FL
BLOOMINGDALE'S, New York, NY

HENRI BENDEL, New York, NY
WOODWARD & LOTHROP, Washington, DC
NICKELS, Owing Mills, MD
EXECUTIVE LEVEL, CARSONS, Chicago, IL
ROCOCO, Pikesville, MD

ITOKIN PLAZA, King of Prussia, PA
GANTOS, Milwaukee, WI
LUNA, Bal Harbour, FL
ORMOND, Dothan, AL
ROBERT PHILLIPS, Beverly Hills, CA

MANO A MANO, New York, NY
EXECUTIVE LEVEL, CARSONS, Chicago, IL
BONWIT TELLER, New York, NY
BEAU BRUMMEL, New York, NY
TOMMY HILFIGER, New York, NY

POLITIX, Los Angeles, CA
TOP MAN, London & Watford, England
ESPRIT, Los Angeles, CA
EXPRESS, New York, NY
FIZZAZZ, New York, NY

METROPOLIS ON 2, CARSONS, Chicago, IL
WILKES SPORT, San Fran./Newport Bch., CA
JESS, Los Angeles, CA
STEFANEL, Los Angeles, CA
GOLDI, Schaumberg, IL

LEVENTHAL SHOES, Woodbury, NY
9 WEST, Ann Arbor, MI

TROPAZ, Willowbrook, NJ
BORSHEIMS, Omaha, NE
ETAGE, Tampa, FL

ACCESSORY PLACE, Livingston, NJ
IPCO SUPER OPTICAL, Lakewood, CO
PRECISION LENSCRAFTERS, Pittsburgh, PA
KOALA BLUE, Costa Mesa, CA
WEATHER STORE, New York, NY

GEAR, New York, NY
LEVEL 6, CARSONS, Chicago, IL
DANIEL HECHTER, New York, NY
COMPANY STORE, Minneapolis, MN
NEXT, London, England

THINK BIG, New York, NY
TRAVELING LIGHT, Los Angeles, CA
NORTH FACE, Costa Mesa, CA
PACIFIC MOTION, Colorado Springs, CO
HEAD, Denver, CO

KRON CHOCOLATIER, Great Neck, NY
CRABTREE & EVELYN, Escondido, CA
RECORD WORLD, Garden City, NY
BLOOMIE'S EXPRESS, JFK Airport, NY
LA SAMARITAINE, Paris, France

PARISIAN, Hoover, AL
BROADWAY, Costa Mesa, CA
HECHT'S, Washington, DC
SAKS, Palm Springs, CA
HESS, Poughkeepsie, NY

NORDSTROM, Costa Mesa, CA
ISETAN, Tokyo, Japan
HOUSE OF FRASIER, London, England
LEWIS, Leeds, England

RETAIL REPORTING 101 Fifth Avenue, New York, N.Y. 10003

15
Office Supplies

Our Stationery Store is either the very old-fashioned kind—or the very newest kind. It has everything: the daily newspaper—in several languages,—magazines on every subject, books, maps, travel guides, posters, greeting cards, school supplies, office supplies,—and party supplies. It has everything from paper plates and party cups to confetti to reams of typing paper to ruled lesson books. You may have to extend your search to find one store that contains office supplies as well as the desks, the files—and file drawers, the chairs that swivel, spin and tilt,—the stat machines and the computer equipment.

In this store we find the decorative wherewithal for children's party settings, for outdoor picnics, Fourth of July celebrations, summer outings to the park or the beach,—for Back to School and Back to College—Career Dressing—dorm rooms, study halls, libraries and more. Since the examples that follow do explain what can be accomplished with what,—let us review some other sources of supply for similar merchandise.

The Carnival Suppliers who have everything from the games—the wheels of fortune—the weighing scales—the kewpie dolls and stuffed animals—to the colorful tents, counters, and strings of colored lights.

Airline and Travel Agencies: the AAA and other Travel clubs for posters, maps, trip-strips, graphics,—maybe even models of planes or trains for travel-oriented displays. Along the same line: The Tourist Bureaus of the various States in the United States—and the many foreign countries who do have many "give-aways" that can tell an Import or Designer story or promote a product.

Not quite computers—and the Computer Stores are spreading rapidly—but the Electronic Games Suppliers—usually for rentals. The glorified "slot machines" are full of color, excitement and "Take a Chance" on a "Sure Winner"—and they provide action and illuminated graphics that hurry and scurry across the darkened screen.

Posters and Broadsheets make excellent backgrounds for display areas. In addition to the travel posters and the posters of Rock Stars—Soap Stars or Movie Heros and Heroines, there are the Movie and Theater posters—the Opera, Ballet and Concert Hall announcements. Contact the theater—the Opera House or the Ballet company and see if you can't also borrow some of their unused costumes to use in your display. It really is a lot of free advertising space for them. And,—don't forget the local thesbians. It may be the college production of a classic—or a review—, it can be the high school's production of "South Pacific" or the All-City Band concert. Those posters can and will give meaning to a window display if cleverly integrated with the merchandise. The traveling RCA or Columbia Artists are always looking for auspicious places to show off their noted artists. Maybe you can combine the posters with some of the instruments from the Music Store?

For rather unusual posters try your local Historical Societies-Museums—or Libraries. They may have some oldies that are real goodies for an anniversary promotion or a Founder's Day sale.

If you pursue it, you should be able to find out who puts up all those big broadsheets on the outdoor signboards around town and out of town. They are window background size—easy to staple up and remove for great getting-attention—out in the street.

RALPH LAUREN, POLO, Madison Avenue, New York City
Corp. Head of Creative Services: **Jeff Walker**

167

ROSSETTI, Madison Avenue, New York City
Window Design: **Chuck Price**

Yesterday's News can be tomorrow's display. Nobody can get close enough to actually read the headlines but the printed matter is the message. "It's the News"—"In Black and White"—"All the Pattern that's Fit To Print"—"Everybody is Talking About ____". Newspapers can be spread out to cover a floor—can line a wall or even be tied back as drapes. They can be piled up as elevations for accessory lay downs or to provide seats for mannequins—or steps for figures that are "In Step with the News". Daily newspapers can be collaged into SALE letters that have immediacy and impact—or cut out and applied against the front glass to mask a window with only a burst left through which the shoppers can view the special merchandise presentation behind. You can even upholster furniture with newspapers—and use them as "unwrappings" for a display of China and glass.

The kind of newspaper you use also proclaims the kind of merchandise you're presenting. French and Italian dailies tucked under mannequins' arms or spread open to be read can easily express an Import theme of foreign fashions. Chinese and Japanese papers could "wrap" small decorative bibelots from abroad. You can also add the crates—the excelsior and the stencilled message to the display. Most people—even people who have never seen a copy—know what Wall St. Journal stands for—and the prestige, and dignity it adds to the "Man on the way up" or in "Blue Chip Clothes" that are an "Investment in Style". The Journal is the ultimate in business—and business suits—and traditional wear. When the styling calls for a tongue-in-cheek approach—something sensational— glitzy—campy or downright trashy—you can order in a few copies of The Enquirer or The Star—in plain brown wrappers.

So,—Newspapers: read them—roll them up and dress them up—spread them out—paste or plaster them on walls—make them into "head-liners" to wear bowties and hats. There are so many ways of Spread out Yesterday's news.

ADDISON-ON-MADISON, New York City
Window Design: **Kurt Schuster**

CERRUTTI, Madison Avenue, New York City
Window Design: Gaylord

Reams of clean white typing paper can be stacked up into steps or swirled into a spiral stairway for small fashion accents. The sheets of typing paper can be curled—crimped—cut—or even folded origami style into small sailboats—soldier hats—airplanes—birds—butterflies and exotic animals. "File this under Fashion"—either on metal or wood in-out trays in myriad styles and colors, or in the accordian folded folders lettered to suit the occasion—and the merchandise.

To travel—or to suggest Import—or items worth studying—there are maps—road maps—globes—atlases and more books on where and how to go. The large maps can be unfurled across a backwall or mounted onto foamcore to become a back-up panel for fashions that are all set to go. A few pieces of your own or borrowed luggage could fill in the foreground. Small shadow boxes can be lined with easy to recognize maps in the familiar seas of blue—mountains of gold and yellow—and forests of green. Spin a globe and add a few leather bound books for a class presentation of "Well Educated"—"Smart"—"Head of the Class" accessories.

NORTH BEACH LEATHER, Madison Avenue, New York City
Window Design: David Bradescu

GUCCI, Fifth Avenue, New York City
Corp. Dir. of Visual Presentation: Guy Scarangello

GUCCI, Fifth Avenue, New York City
Corp. Dir. of Visual Presentation: Guy Scarangello

B. ALTMAN, Fifth Avenue, New York City
Window Manager: Andrew Druschilowsky
Window Design: David Milutin

TELLO'S, Arsenal Mall, Watertown, MA
Window Director: Kathy Shing

GIMBELS, New York
V.M. Director: Bernie Hauserman

MACY'S, Herald Square, New York City
Window Manager: Linda Fargo

JORDAN MARSH, Boston, MA
V.M. Director: Robert Unger, V.P.

In the Party Supply Section there is fun and excitement in the form of honey-combed tissue bells and balls—streamers and confetti—dominos and devilish devices—horns and hats—lanterns and lampooning masks. There are the papergoods in bright and pastel colors—plates of all sizes—cups and "glasses"—napkins and tablecloths—to crush—to crumple—to toss about with abandon. Confetti and streamers madly swirling, snaking and uncoiling through a display area can just as easily ring in the New Year's Eve and a show of fabulous ball gowns (maybe with dominos—and fancy masks)—as become a ship's send off—a Bon Voyage cascade for cruise and resort wear—setting off for an adventure filled holiday. In the Jourdan display, the party takes on a patriotic note to celebrate red, white and blue swimwear topped with diamond dusted paper top hats.

The wedding setting is a tumble of delicate white honey-combed bells made to appear elegant and refined in the subdued light. They provide an almost bower-like back up for the gowns.

SILHOUETTE, Washington, DC
Design: Prop—John Kiser

MACY'S, Herald Square, New York City
Window Manager: Linda Fargo

Party hats can be part of a costume—or just accentuate an attitude. These stacked up, shaped cloth derbies provide a Gay 90s touch to an outfit that has a "vested back interest"—and the hats also play up the black and white theme of the window and the outfit. Imagine what you could do with party hats and children's wear—anything from play clothes to party clothes. They are just right—and some confetti and streamers couldn't hurt. The derby plus a graphic cutout of a handlebar moustache could be all one would need for Father's Day—unless you topped each mannequin with a derby and stuck on an obvious fake moustachio.

Akari—Oriental lanterns—assorted sizes and shapes from white balls to snaky floor to ceiling tubes can add texture—design—and LIGHT to a composition. At Silhouette, they are a handsome addition to a black and white window presentation and they fill in the background—provide a separation from the selling floor—add sparkle and a festive quality to the setting. It's "Party Time"—"Let's Have Fun"—"Light Up the Night"—with Akari.

SAGE ALLEN, Hartford, CT
V.M. Director: Stephen Delgizzo

The office supply houses can keep your windows propped for most of the year—without running out of "idea" supplies. Computers are almost as popular as T.V. monitors. They too get the shopper to stop and watch the strange messages flashing across the dark screens. You could even program your own message! For annual occurences like Back to School, Back to College, and Career Dressing,—computers are compatible with the fashions and provide vignette settings that don't require much more to make the scene. For prints and patterns—the punny "Print Explosion" paid off royally as an attention getter for the patterned merchandise strung out across the back wall of Filene's window. Stat machines can be office settings for black/white fashion or even colored with the new, color capable machines. "Print it"—"Black on White"—"Line for Line Copies"—"Something for Everyone".

If metal file drawers and desks can move out into the open for picnics and outdoor living—imagine what they can do indoors for an office setting—a school setting—a study in a dorm. "Find Fashion filed under _____", "Take a letter"—and all these pieces come in technicolor!

FILENE'S, Boston, MA
V.M. Director: Vincent Vitolo
Boston Visuals Director: Steven Vieser

KAUFMANN'S, Pittsburgh, PA
V.M. Director: David Knouse, V.P.
Downtown Visual Director: Anthony Lucas

16
Toys and Models

Try a toy store like an F.A.O. Schwartz where every childhood fantasy becomes a reality and so many display ideas and plans can also become a reality. As you peruse the next several pages you will see just a few things that can be done with everybody's favorite toy—the Teddy Bear—and its big family of stuffed, plush animals that children will unabashedly carress, hug and squeeze and even adult males will furtively stroke or pet. They do bring with them a sense of innocence—or security—or special memories of the past. People will stop to look at the furry beings and smile back at their animated antics. No one is ever too old for a soft, cuddly toy and no gown ever gets too formal that it can't be accompanied by a bow-tied bear or an oversized plush penguin.

Models and miniatures; from railroad trains, shown on the left, to model cars, planes and trucks. They provide scale, interest and humor to a display. That's what much of this store's merchandise is all about; humor, smiles, fond and happy memories. Ride your small accessories out on cars and trucks,—scoop up baubles and beads with miniature shovels,—raise up a scarf or belt caught in the teeth of a yellow crane operating from a toy truck,—or go off to war in khaki—in brass—or in insignias in small but mighty jeeps, tanks and camouflaged trucks. You might even add a G.I. Joe. Going traveling—or promoting luggage? Fill your friendly display sky with models of airplanes of wood, plastic or metal.

Think of "All the Right Moves" you can make with Board Games. "Monopolize" a fashion trend— "Pick one—or two",—"Go to——", "You Win!". The truth is,—you can't lose with these familiar favorites. A simple line-drawing or grafitti sketch along with "Pictionary" and your viewers will figure out the word. "Go to The Head of the Class"—"We've Got the Answers"—"Don't Leave it to Chance".

We mentioned in another chapter the beach inflatables—and all the other plastic toys found in a toy store, so let's turn to the hundreds of things you can do with the materials to be found at the Magic counter where the sleight-of-hand stuff turns into display props; the endless string of colored scarves,—the feather flower bouquet,—the top hat waiting to be emptied of all the fashion accessories that are crammed inside. "Cut" the mannequin in half—or "saw" her in two—if you are showing separates—"These Go Together". Or try the same act with shoes and boots as the featured merchandise.

We should mention the computer games—the oversized animals—the undersized replicas of sporty sportscars—the four foot tall Raggedy Anns and Andys and the host of dolls of all sizes, colors and national dress (for Imports). There are the Lego sets and the Lincoln Logs with which to build structures in shadow boxes or cases—and the playhouses and cardboard constructed castles that are kid scaled but will serve for Milady's bower or tower on Valentine's Day.

You'll need a long pad and a very big shopping cart to satisfy your "I want" list as you go through the Toy and Model store.

SAKS FIFTH AVENUE, New York City
Visual Merchandising Director: **Michael Keith, V.P.**
New York Window Director: **Roger Jones**

Kidding around! Whether it's little kids playing at being grown up or grown ups letting the fashion accessories play it out with kid's toy and miniature models—whatever —it works! Saks on page 176 did a Christmas spectacular with a spectacular model train set-up in a Victorian setting, that raced and chugged through four main windows to standing room crowds of viewers—with kids in the "mezzanine"—on daddy's shoulders. It had motion lights—and brought back fond memories of childhood. On these pages: rugged steel truck models plow their way over coarse salt snow to pick up the interest in the winter boots and bags being featured. A "Moving Sale" got more than its share of viewing—and smiles—as the miniature movers took one shoe at a time across an otherwise untrimmed window. In the left corner: a pile up of shoes, bags, and scarves waiting to be picked up and delivered.

The train tracks assure you that you are on the right track—fashionwise with Fendi bags. On the wall: the tracks are laid out in the familiar Fendi logo—and small leather accessories are side-tracked above—in the spotlight. Detoured—but not forgotten.

MARIO VALENTINO, New York City

I. MILLER, Fifth Avenue, New York City
Window Design: **Howard Nevelow**

BERGDORF GOODMAN, New York City
Director of Design: **Angela Patterson, V.P.**

STEVEN E., Great Neck, NY
Window Design: Mindy Greenberg

CERRUTTI, Madison Avenue, New York City
Window Design: Gaylord

On Target! Darts that make a perfect fashion hit—that scores high—and even color coordinates with the black and red merchandise being featured. The mannequin's head is hidden behind the dart board while the darts seem to be flying everywhere—striking the garments for points. This open back window makes use of the glass block cash/wrap desk behind to elevate one of the casually clad mannequins.

There are so many simple, inexpensive and amusing toys and games waiting to be played in the displays. For an urban setting: colored plastic paddles add dash to the yellow, black and white separates—and the long stretches of rubber bands are tangled. They may miss hitting the ball but they are a hit in the window.

GIMBELS, New York City
V.M. Director: Bernie Hauserman

JORDAN MARSH, Boston, MA
V.M. Director: Linda Bramlage, V.P.

Blow it up! Inflatables pack and store flat but can blow up into full size window display props. Starting with swimwear —and down on the beach there are beach balls—toys— rafts—sunning mattresses—life-savers—floats—pillows— fish and deepsea monsters—even palm trees to fill in the setting. Dinosaurs are now available from mini to maxi—to add interest or shock to a window presentation. Look around the toy and novelty shops for all the other fabulous inflatables that abound.

The most familiar and probably the favorite of all favorite inflatables are the good, old-fashioned balloons. No party, celebration, anniversary, political campaign or send-off would be complete without these high-flying, colorful, bright balls of rubber that add so much for so little. You do have to watch them—in the heated windows—and maybe replace some that start to sag or wrinkle—but they put on a great show while they last. Bring them inside the store and let the party go on and on.

Everybody's favorite toy. Cuddlesome—caressable—warm and tender—stuffed teddys—stuffed plushy anything gets ohs and ahs from little kids—and big kids. Ladies in formalwear—in lacy lingerie or flannel pajamas bring them along for security—and a smile. They can be dressed up in shirts and sweaters, perched on stools and sell a range of color coordinated merchandise to men and women. They also look great in Tees—and in shorts—they will wear ties —necklaces—scarves—even earrings. Try them in shoes—high heels or flats. They are the ''bare-facts'' and ''snuggle perfect''—and are sure to get the viewer's eye when head above shoulders of a pinned up or hung up outfit. So many stores are now using these plushy pets as Christmas gifts with purchase—or purchase with purchase—so why not let them also prop your holiday windows and interiors. If your store doesn't carry any stuffed animals in stock,—they may be in the nearest ''zoo'' only doors away waiting to make a window appearance.

COURREGES, New York City

SAGE-ALLEN, Hartford, CT
V.M. Director: **Stephen Delgizzo**

OLIVERS, New York City
Visuals Sitarski/Heneks

17
Display Props

This volume could be called a Dictionary or Encyclopedia of Cliches,—of the usual, the expected and the mundane. We prefer to think of these cliches as a form of Graphic Communication; a foolproof way of telling our customers something in a glance—without words or long descriptions. When a viewer sees a column or a pediment, she knows immediately that the merchandise besides the prop is classic—it is elegant—it has lasting value. We don't have to say it. The dimensional objects have already spoken. A pyramid means "permanence"—a fish "says" water and swimwear,—a single park bench makes a park or all outdoors.

Sometimes the displayperson wants to be more emphatic—make a larger than life statement and that is when the Display manufacturers and distributors—the makers and shapers of the unusual—the unique—and the special props are eagerly sought for and their lines are studied with interest. A two foot inflatable ball can be great fun, but imagine rolling in a six foot diameter one coated in shiny lacquer. There is no doubt that many everyday objects do yeoman service and more in display, but the occasional blast of the oversized—the overscaled—the "outrageous"—the "awesome" interpretation of the usual will work display wonders.

There is no way we can either list the hundreds of suppliers or manufacturers here in the United States—or across Europe or in the Orient,—or even attempt to itemize the many marvels they produce. Our recommendations are simple—and effective. Visit the trade shows and the bi-annual and annual exhibits of the Visual Merchandising and Display industry. Come to see what is new twice each year as the National Association of Display Industries spreads out over more and more space in the public exhibition palaces—and as the showrooms proliferate in and around New York City. You are always guaranteed a fine show and a full viewing of new products—props and surprises. Each year, out in San Francisco, the West Coast Visual Merchandisers (W.A.V.M.) put on a gala presentation of tasteful materials in idea-crammed spaces for the pleasurable perusal by displaypersons looking for "something new and different". Once every three years a Hypermarket of Visual Merchandising, Display and Store Design is created out in Dusseldorf where, over acres and acres of land, thousands of products are spread out for four days of intensive studying—and shopping. What a toy store is to a toyless kid this show is to a displayperson seeking props.

There are also publications—trade magazines that are rich in ads—with open invitations to write in for booklets, brochures and/or catalogues. Most of these companies are members of either the N.A.D.I. or the W.A.V.M.—and they can be counted on to produce what they promise.

What we conclude with here are only very, very few of the many, many special props that have no "period" or "time"—but go on and on serving the imaginative displayperson—as the seasons go by and the years go by—so long as the displayperson adapts them to new uses and new promotions.

CYXTYZ, Los Angeles, CA
Window Design: **R.J.M. Studio, Los Angeles, CA**
Photo: **Ted Buel, Los Angeles, CA**

VITTORIO RICCI, Madison Avenue, New York City
Window Design: Marc Manigault

Picture frames that are overscaled for big fashion statements even when the merchandise offerings are small and precious. Often the vacuum formed, light weight and bright gold frames can outline a window as an ornate proscenium —or just become a fragmented proscenium within a window—enriched with striped or damasked fabric that pulls back to reveal an array of fine gifts. The acanthus leaf corbels, on the wall, support individual place settings but could as easily support a shelf between them and a whole line of china. The frames and sections of frames used in the Vittorio Ricci window manage to tame a tall window and subdivide it into convenient viewing vistas for elegant, party-going, shoes and bags. A swath of gold lame fabric leads from the top frames—through the lower frame and cascades out onto the checkered floor.

WOODWARD & LOTHROP, Washington, DC
Div. V.P. Visual Merchandising: Jack Domer
Washington V.M. Director: Jan Suit

MARSHALL FIELD, Chicago, IL
V.M. Director: Homer Sharp, S.V.M.

Architectural elements can say so much about the merchandise. These obelisks are clustered into a single composition to sell classically traditional coats and suits. A single obelisk would just as effectively provide the vertical elegance for a dinner dress—ball gown—lingerie—or furs—or career oriented suits for men or women. The obelisk is classic; it suggests strength—dignity—a lasting quality—not one soon to disappear. These lightweight, mache models can bring these same attributes into the store on a platform—or ledge—in front of a boutique or designer shop—where they can be seen "full round".

LAZARUS, Dayton, OH
V.M. Director: Kurt Millikin

JORDAN MARSH, Boston, MA
V.M. Director: Robert Unger, V.P.

It must be obvious to all that the classic of classic elements are the capitol and the columns—the pediments and pedestals that are Doric—Ionic—or Corinthian—in go-with-anything white—neutraled to granite gray—or gilded for fashionable exposure. The capitols are available with or without the columns and as shown on this page: the caps can cap off a mannequin—topple under the weight of a designer's name or stand up to hold up a suit form or a pile of pillows. The columns can add vertical dignity to a presentation—or cut into sections, provide elevations for sitting or merchandise lay downs.

MACY'S, Herald Square, New York City
Window Manager: Linda Fargo

Dressforms don't have to be dressed and all hidden to make an image statement. Just to see the traditional canvas covered form—with or without the upholstered head and the added-on wooden articulated arms—makes the viewer know that something is "Hand Made"—"Couture Design"—out of an atelier or studio—"Especially Fashioned"—"Fitted to Order". There is snob appeal inherent in the dressform—a unique, one-of-a-kind attitude that gets across to the viewer. In both of these examples, the form serves to show the accessories rather than the suit or dress one could expect to see. The Barneys window shows a complete gamut of accents: a hat precariously perched on the gilded knob of the neck plate—a scarf is jauntily arranged over the shoulders—a choice of belts— gloves, bracelet and bangles in hand and on the wrist—a small bag slung from the shoulder and—on the floor: shoes, bag and even an umbrella. A masterful job of display—and display lighting.

The Bloomingdale's window features Fendi bags and the figures are loaded down with the patterned fabric bags while, on the antique sewing machine—a wooden artists mannequin is stitching away on more of the same.

BLOOMINGDALE'S, Lexington Avenue, New York City
V.M. Director: **Colin Birch**
BARNEYS, Chelsea, New York City
Creative Director: **Simon Doonan**

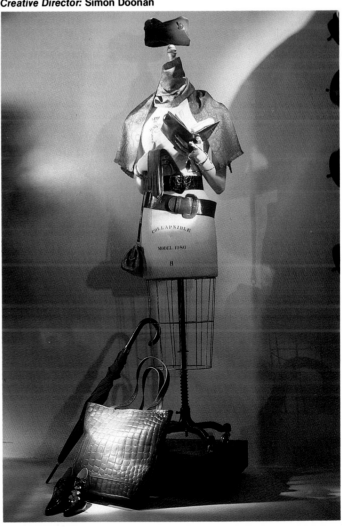

WOODWARD & LOTHROP, Washington, DC
Div. V.P. Visual Merchandising: Jack Dorner
Washington V.M. Director: Jan Suit

PIERRE CARDIN, New York Ctiy

There are so many materials available through the Display manufacturers and suppliers. Some we just take for granted and never think of as vital to getting the job done. Seamless paper is a "standard"—a standby—a must! The color range grows and the wide, unbroken widths cover backgrounds—rip—shred—tear—crush and crumple to suit the suit or to satisfy the color needs of the display.

Scale—especially overscale gets attention and creates immediate interest in what is being offered. Display manufacturers excel in producing infinite, giant—heroic-sized everyday objects that can be like building blocks to the professional and imaginative visual merchandiser/displayperson. The objects can be recolored—grouped or clustered or singled out as the display concept may warrant. The big shapes reach out from the window to bring the viewer over to eye the smaller obects below. Right: Christmas ornaments that fill a display area with color but can be converted to stylized world globes for travel or Import promotions—"balloons" for kids wear and monster celebrations—coated with diamond-dust snow to become snowballs or be built into snowmen for windows and ledges—and on and on. As that old song goes—"Use Your Imagination". Isn't that what display is all about?

JOSLINS, Denver, CO
V.M. Director: Ron Gosses

Index of Stores